A Path of Their Own

Helping Children to Educate Themselves

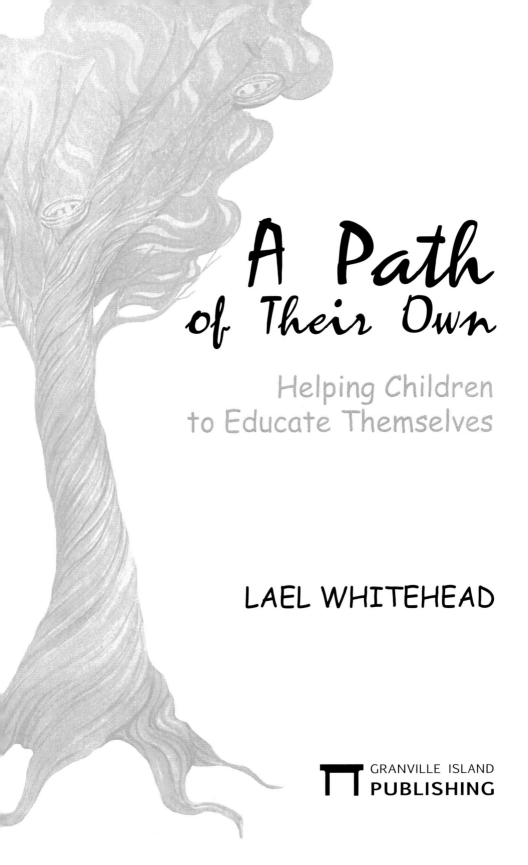

A Path
of Their Own

Helping Children
to Educate Themselves

LAEL WHITEHEAD

GRANVILLE ISLAND
PUBLISHING

Library and Archives Canada Cataloguing in Publication

Whitehead, Lael, 1960-, author
    A path of their own : helping children to educate themselves / Lael Whitehead.

Includes bibliographical references and index.
ISBN 978-1-926991-39-9 (pbk.)

    1. Home schooling. 2. Self-culture. 3. Parenting. 4. Love.
5. Respect. 6. Compassion. 7. Whitehead, Lael, 1960-. I. Title.

LC40.W45 2013   371.04'2   C2013-906123-1

Copy editor: Renate Preuss
Cover and text designer: Omar Gallegos
Cover art: Julia Iredale
Indexing: Bookmark: Editing & Indexing

Granville Island Publishing Ltd.
212 – 1656 Duranleau St.
Vancouver, BC, Canada V6H 3S4

604-688-0320 / 1-877-688-0320
info@granvilleislandpublishing.com
www.granvilleislandpublishing.com

First published in May 2014
Printed in Canada on recycled paper

Also available as an E-book
ISBN 978-1-926991-56-6

For Richard,
fellow traveller and best friend

Acknowledgements

I would like to thank my mother, Lorita, my father, Lee, and my stepmother, Pegeen, for their help with fine-tuning my manuscript and for all their support and encouragement over the years. They have modeled for me how to live with integrity, kindness and courage. I feel incredibly blessed to have them in my life. I am grateful too for the wonderful Vancouver Homelearners' Association that I was part of in the early years of our unschooling journey, and for the homelearning friends I have met in Victoria. If it weren't for the support of these brave and inspiring companions, I would have found it hard to persist in taking the road less travelled. Thanks, too, to Jo Blackmore and her crew at Granville Island Publishing for their many helpful suggestions, and for their expertise.

I cannot adequately express my gratitude to my family. My three daughters have been my "spirit guides." Their playfulness, curiosity and passion continually inspire me to engage more fully with my own life. They each took time from their busy lives to write articles for this book, at my request. Richard, my best friend for over thirty years, has walked every twist and turn of the road alongside me, sharing each challenge and each new discovery on the way. He has believed in this book even when I wanted to abandon the project, read countless drafts as I developed it and also contributed an essay to the manuscript. His optimism and good humour have been the best support of all.

Thank you, Life, for these gifts.

Contents

Acknowledgements   vii

Foreword by Wendy Priesnitz   xi

Preface   xv

Introduction
The Way of Radical Respect   xvii

Chapter One
Beginnings   1

Chapter Two
Questioning the Paradigm   15

Chapter Three
The Paradigm Shifts   25

Chapter Four
The Language of Power   35

Chapter Five
Finding the Jewel   43

Insert 1
Finding the Inner Voice   59

Chapter Six
Curriculum: See How They Run!   63

Chapter Seven
Play   73

Chapter Eight
The Three Rs   81

Insert 2
Designing a Life Worth Living   89

Chapter Nine
The Socialization Question   95

Chapter Ten
Our Year in Sports   101

Chapter Eleven
Journaling: A Tool for Self-Discovery   107

Chapter Twelve
Ordinary Genius   111

Chapter Thirteen
Fallow Times   117

Insert 3
The Unhurried Mind   123

Chapter Fourteen
Siblings   131

Chapter Fifteen
Sexuality and Other Awakenings   135

Chapter Sixteen
Sharing the Journey   141

Chapter Seventeen
Holding Until Relaxed   149

Insert 4
Art as Magic   159

Chapter Eighteen
Conscious Leadership   163

Chapter Nineteen
The Emptying Nest   173

Afterword
Some Abiding Questions   177

Notes   183

Index   187

Foreword

When I was a young mother in the early 1970s, I was determined to raise our two daughters with the respect and trust that I hadn't received as a child. I didn't know exactly what that would look like, but we began by breastfeeding, which seemed obvious to me but not to my mother or our doctor. We co-slept, and my husband and I carried our babies everywhere. Even before they were born, we had agreed that our children would be able to avoid the regimentation, coercion, distrust and creativity-stifling monotony that were part of compulsory schooling; we knew their intrinsic motivation and curiosity, along with the richness of everyday life, would propel them to learn whatever they needed. And soon, our trust in their developing ability to self-manage was being extended into other aspects of life, such as bedtimes, clothing, friendships and food. Our lifestyle was unusual in those days, and we were largely without support or information, with few models or even books to guide us.

Some aspects of that life were more public, and more controversial, than others. Learning without school certainly fell into that category. Soon, I found myself educating the educators about homeschooling's legality — defending, advocating and, ultimately, organizing. I used the platform of *Natural Life Magazine*, which our family had begun as a way of supporting ourselves and our home-based learning lifestyle, to launch a national homeschooling alliance in 1979. I prodded others to start more local support groups, conducted some research, spoke with the media and wrote a book.

I thought that elements of our lifestyle would become common in a decade or two. I assumed that I would be able to stop talking and writing about the need to make conscious choices about more respectful parenting, education reform, environmental stewardship, and the like. However, just the opposite seems to have happened. Although those of us who care about such things aren't as lonely as we were forty years ago, mainstream attitudes still make those ideas seem radical.

"Radical" is a word that I didn't used to like. It conjured up images of rebellion and revolution, which I thought would scare people away from exploring some of the choices I think we need to make if our families, communities and planet are to flourish (to survive, even). But now I realize that we need a paradigm shake-up of that scale. So I share with my readers that the word "radical" comes from the Latin word *radicalis*, which means having roots; the botanical term "radical leaves" refers to leaves that arise from the root or crown of the plant. So "radical" simply means examining the roots of an issue. And a radical solution to a problem is one that arises from that examination, addressing the root cause, rather than more superficial symptoms.

And that's what this book does, whether we are thinking about the problems we experience in education, in parenthood or in other aspects of living on this earth. Lael Whitehead — with her relentless questioning, her strong belief in children and in life, her brave mind and open heart — has written a testament to how respecting children can lead to a radical and restorative change in how we live, one that is kinder, gentler, more thoughtful and more life-affirming.

We need this inspiration, perhaps more now than ever. We need the thoughtful companionship found here to help us along the path of learning and living as if school doesn't exist. We need the reassurance and confidence that come from reading stories like this. There are many lessons to be learned from this family that lived with children in respect and dignity, protecting and nurturing their individual natures (and from the self-described "mistakes" they made along the way). And we can be grateful for the stories about the thriving, happy young people — the "ordinary geniuses" — those children grew up to be.

Wendy Priesnitz, Toronto, Canada, 2013

Wendy Priesnitz is the editor of *Life Learning Magazine*. She is also the author of *School Free, Challenging Assumptions in Education* and *Beyond School: Living As If School Doesn't Exist*.

Preface

Nothing you become will disappoint me. I have no preconception that I'd like to see you be or do. I have no desire to foresee you, only to discover you. [1]

Mary Haskell, in a letter to Kahlil Gibran

When I first decided to write this book, I thought it would be about "education." I figured my job was simply to describe how my three children grew up and became skillful, adept human beings without formal schooling. But I have come to realize that education is not the central issue. The issue is love. Talking about learning without talking about love is like trying to construct a building without starting on the ground floor. Relationships are our starting place, the soil we grow in. The emotional environment children encounter in their early years becomes the foundation for their future lives; whether they become curious, creative and compassionate adults, who care about others and about the planet they live on, hinges on how they were treated from the beginning.

"To school or not to school" is not the real question. Instead, I want to ask in this book, "How can we become more loving?" In particular, how can we love our children so that they will blossom to their full human potential? Children are born eager for life. They arrive open and curious, ready to taste, touch and explore everything they encounter. How can we, as parents and mentors, protect this tender openness? How can we relate to our children in a way that enhances and enriches life for us all?

I believe that children — and all people for that matter — *thrive* when they are seen without judgment, when they are accepted as they are. Fear of judgment creates anxiety and tension. Frightened people contract and withdraw, seeking to avoid hurt. They shut down rather than open up to life. In contrast, loving acceptance — or what I will later call "radical respect" — creates an atmosphere of emotional safety. When we feel safe we flourish, both emotionally and intellectually; we reach out, we experiment and take risks, we explore and learn. Learning and love turn out to be two sides of the same coin.

Although I have titled this book *A Path of Their Own*, I believe passionately that we need each other's support and companionship in order to thrive. We are each unique. Each child is born with her or his own set of characteristics and inclinations and curiosities. But each child grows up in a social environment that shapes these innate traits. Children are either helped to find their own wonderful route into the heart of life, or thwarted at every turn by the world that greets them.

We desperately need to redesign our communities so that they become places that foster loving relationships. I believe our very survival may be at stake. Not only our ability to flourish as human beings, but the health of the planet as a whole, depends on our ability to love. We will become good guardians of the earth only when we have cultivated our capacity for respect. *The way we treat one another is how we treat all life.* Our human interdependence is just a small mirror of the interdependence of all creatures on our planet. For better or for worse, we are all in this together.

Introduction

The Way of Radical Respect

Those who think to win the world
By doing something to it,
I see them come to grief.
For the world is a sacred object.
Nothing is to be done to it.
To do anything to it is to damage it.
To seize it is to lose it. [2]

Lao Tsu

I am sitting by the window of my upstairs study, looking out over the sheep fields towards the bay. The house around me is empty and quiet. The children, who once filled the rooms and hallways with their chatter, their running footsteps, their bickering, their delighted play, have all grown up. If I squint just a little, I almost glimpse a small girl running downhill across the grass away from me. Her long fair hair flies out behind her. Her feet lift high into the air with each springing step. She is so eager to run, so keen to explore what is far away out of sight in the trees. Who is it? Lauren? Marlise? Julia? But the girlish ghost is gone and the winter field returns to stillness.

My three grown daughters have asked me to write this book. They have urged me to put my ideas on paper, and have given me permission to tell their stories. Lauren, who is now pregnant with her first child, wants to be able to give this book to some of her friends who have children. She lives in an alternative community, where young families are committed to living sustainably, to growing and eating organic food, and to using up less of the world's resources. However, Lauren is often shocked to see how easily her friends fall back into age-old habits of domination and coercion when it comes to raising their children. They give "time-outs" and rewards in order to enforce compliant behaviour, without thinking about the world they are modeling for their kids. She believes that there is little hope for our planet unless human beings can learn to treat one another differently.

At first I hesitated to write a book. I believe passionately in the maxim "live and let live" and I do not want to give advice or meddle in others' lives. I believe that each life journey yields its gifts and its lessons. There is no right or universal path. But I have also come to believe that each voice is part of an ongoing human conversation, a shared exploration of how to live well. We need to speak out about what matters and to share our discoveries. We learn by listening to one another.

So, with a desire to share what I have learned during my twenty-seven years of mothering, I have re-read my old journals, opened dusty albums of photographs and children's artwork, and tried to retrace my journey. Since I have always been the kind of person who doesn't look back, this has been a strange process. Reviewing the journals I wrote during the many years my children learned at home and out in the world rather than inside schools has been a bit like putting on a favourite old dress, unworn for years. I have had to revisit the challenges, the hopes and the fears our family faced over two decades ago, when we decided to choose the road less travelled. The intense anxiety I felt in the early days — the fear of being different, the worry that I was making a big mistake — seems very far away now. Life has moved on. My daughters are now making their way in the world with grace and power. Although I remain deeply connected with my children, I no longer identify very much with the role of "mother." Instead I am pursuing my own creative path, often inspired by my daughters' example. Looking back has reminded me that I would not be who I am today if it weren't for the road I have travelled.

One of the early working titles for this book was "Of Love and Learning: a memoir of raising children with radical respect." Relationships, I have come to believe, matter profoundly. In fact, whether or not children grow up to be adults capable of creativity and resilience has far more to do with the quality of their early emotional connections than with any specialized training they receive during childhood. Everything in life flows from how we see, and are seen by, each other.

What kinds of relationships help children flourish? Most people would agree that a child needs to be loved in order to be able both to love herself and the world. Most of us sense that the capacity to love is a prerequisite for blossoming to one's full potential, whether intellectual, artistic or social. But the word "love" can mean many things. Possessiveness, control, manipulation and intimidation have all passed for love at one time or another. Domineering parents, for instance, often consider their brutal tactics "loving" because they are convinced they are acting for the good of the child. But to qualify as the genuine article, love, for me, must be rooted in respect. Respect is what makes love a vehicle of connection, rather than of possession or control. The word "respect" derives from the Latin word *respicere*, meaning to "look at, to behold." To respect another is to behold them, to see them truly. I have added the word "radical" to define the kind of deep respect that is the basis of love, because "radical" derives from the Latin word for "root" and implies a quality that goes to the root of things. *To radically respect another is to see, deeply and fully, the reality of his or her being.* It is an act of profound awareness, of acknowledging what is. It is a beholding beyond any desire to influence or change.

Raising children capable of radically respecting themselves, others, and all other forms of life on the earth around them, requires treating them with such respect from the beginning. This book is a memoir of my own struggle to become radically respectful of my children. I have made many mistakes along the way. I have lost sight of them at times; swept up in my own fears or desires, I have tried to control their behaviour or influence their decisions. But whenever I have come back to the simple and profound act of seeing them as they are, I have been reminded how sweet love feels, both for the giver and the receiver. Such loving heals us and makes us braver and stronger. It makes life worth the effort of living.

Chapter One
Beginnings

I will not follow where the path may lead, but I will go where there is no path, and I will leave a trail. [3]

Muriel Strode

When my first child was born I knew my life was going to change forever. But I didn't suspect *how much.* I didn't know that mothering would oblige me to re-evaluate my own culture. I didn't realize that I would come to question the beliefs that underlie everything we do and say.

My first child, Lauren, was unplanned. Richard and I had just returned from a year of backpacking around Europe and Asia. We had no money, no jobs and no place yet to live when we discovered we were pregnant. I remember being traumatized at the thought of starting a family. We weren't ready! We still had to figure out what we were "going to do with our lives." Both of us had undergraduate university degrees but no career in sight. Even my mother-in-law was anxious. It's the wrong time, she felt. We weren't sufficiently prepared. Of course, I knew I could choose not to have the baby. I am a devout believer in planned parenthood. But I was twenty-five and married and already starting to notice children and babies whenever I passed them. I just couldn't resist the new life growing inside me.

Looking back, I realize I was conflicted about the idea of having a child. I never doubted that I would be a mother. But my family and community believed strongly that women should have careers; as a dedicated feminist I felt I should be independent and self-reliant. Staying home with children seemed old-fashioned at best, a cop-out at worst.

My problem was that, although I had a university degree, I wasn't drawn to any particular career. Richard and I liked to spin scenarios of the lives we could lead but beneath all my fantasizing lay a sense of unease: I felt no ambition to "be someone." The yuppie lifestyle many of my friends were pursuing seemed hollow and unsatisfying, but I couldn't figure out what I wanted to do instead. I was hungering for a place and time and way of being in the world that I had not yet experienced — one that was less materialistic and more rooted in community. I was "homesick for an unknown country," as the French writer Flaubert called it.

Having a child seemed meaningful in a way that the other options open to me at the time did not. I think I was a little ashamed of this feeling. Part of me saw having children as the easy way out. It would immediately give me a role to play, a sense of purpose in life, even though it was one that was not admired any longer by my culture. When I look back on it now, I realize that I felt a strong calling towards motherhood. At some deep level I knew that my heart path lay that way; I sensed that the journey of mothering would be the road to my own flowering as a human being.

When Lauren was born a powerful sense of meaning entered my life. When I first held her in my arms, the world shimmered with aliveness. Here was a whole new universe emerging into being and I was privileged to be the conduit. This luminous stranger was not part of me, but we were intimately and intensely connected to one another. Any thoughts of "what does it all mean?" fell away as I looked at her. It was like gazing at Life itself, and having Life gaze back at me.

I stayed home with her for nine months. Richard enrolled in a three-year graduate program in architecture and was eager to begin a professional career. Gradually, although I loved being with my baby, I began to feel pressured both from within and without to do something with my life other than be an at-home mom. I decided to go back to school, this time for a master's in English. I put Lauren in daycare part-time. I enjoyed the university classes and the reading and the chance to meet other students, but I wasn't nearly as engaged by school as I had been as an undergraduate. My heart and mind were always partly with Lauren. I felt terrible pangs of guilt when I picked her up from daycare and sensed her tension and unhappiness. Though everyone around me assumed it was natural and fitting that I leave my baby to be looked after by others, in my gut I knew the arrangement was not only hard on her, but hard on me. There was an umbilical cord of energy still binding us to one another. When we were apart we both suffered.

When our second daughter, Marlise, was born I had finished the course work for my degree and decided to stay home full-time. I felt relieved that the job of looking after two young children seemed big enough that no one, for the moment, urged me to go to work. But the pressure began to build again. When Marlise was about a year and a half I started to teach English as a second language half-time. That launched a very stressful couple of years of shuttling children between preschool and babysitters. Then I got pregnant with number three, Julia. Living with two small children and a baby was completely overwhelming! Any thought of working outside the home was banished for the time being.

Mostly I loved being at home with my toddlers. Each day was like riding a huge wave of energy — actually many separate smaller waves — that surged through the house. It was messy and noisy and creative and lively. At times, however, I was still plagued by low self-esteem. My friends who had become doctors and lawyers were puzzled that I was choosing to stay at home. I don't know if they meant to be unsupportive, but at times I felt judged and paranoid. I blamed myself for not having more drive to develop a career of my own. Richard was passionate about architecture. Where was my passion?

It wasn't until Lauren was seven and our family made a dramatic choice to "get off the bus" of conventional schooling that I began to discover what had been calling me all these years. Choosing not to send my children to school caused me, for the first time, to take a long, hard look at the values driving the culture around me. I discovered that the "unknown country" I'd been longing for was actually a way of experiencing and valuing the world that had been right in front of me all along. All it took was for me finally to stop waiting for others to give it their seal of approval. I had to learn to stand tall and claim this new country as my own.

I arrived at my unorthodox view of education in a roundabout way. The first time I'd ever heard the term "home schooling" was at our local playground one fall day when Lauren and Marlise were four and two. Lauren had struck up an instant friendship with another girl about her age and the two of them were delightedly chasing each other up and down the playground. The new girl had an older brother, perhaps six or seven, who would occasionally join in their play, between bouts of swinging and sliding on the play equipment. The other mother and I fell to talking. I asked the usual question: where did her son go to school? I was astonished by her answer. He didn't. And he wasn't going to go any time soon. She and her husband had decided to "home school" him. Their plan was to follow an unstructured, child-led curriculum of their own designing.

I had never met anyone who didn't send their kids to school. I was curious and peppered her with questions. Although our conversation was polite and friendly, I was shocked by the idea, even repelled. Growing up without schooling? How would children learn social skills? How would they be exposed to new ideas? How would they avoid becoming emotionally enmeshed with their parents? I couldn't help feeling sorry for the woman and for her two children. Although she seemed nice, there must be something wrong with her or with her husband. Normal parents believed in public education. Perhaps she suffered from anxiety disorder? Perhaps she had experienced some kind of trauma during her own school years that she'd never successfully processed or outgrown?

I walked home from the park with the girls slowly that day, musing over my encounter. Marlise was in the stroller, chattering non-stop and pointing eagerly at every dog, tree or car we passed. Lauren sang as she walked alongside. What exuberant, joyful little beings they were. So unself-conscious and alive! I pictured them going to school. My heart sank immediately. Then I allowed myself, just for a moment, to imagine not sending them. I pictured them growing up to womanhood without the peer pressure and the endless grading and judging that characterize the school environment. Wow! What women they would be — weird, perhaps, but amazingly strong and inner-directed, unconventional and creative. I pushed the thought away. I wasn't a counter-culture type. Stubborn and quietly independent, yes, but not eccentric enough to want to buck the system, or brave enough to weather the negative judgments such an unorthodox choice would provoke.

I forgot about my conversation with the homeschooling mother in the park until several years later. By that time Julia had been born. Lauren was in grade two and Marlise was in her second year of preschool. Life was pretty good. The only problem was that Lauren was miserable.

Lauren didn't like school right from the start. She spent most of the first week of kindergarten in the principal's office because, as she told me, she was "too sad" and couldn't stop crying. Eventually, she adapted to the daily misery and at least withheld her tears until she got home. In grade one she had a new teacher who seemed livelier and more cheerful than the rather dour kindergarten teacher. But Lauren still didn't feel comfortable or safe. I tried everything I could. I volunteered in her classroom every week. We lived only half a block from the school, so she was home for lunch every day. I invited the other little girls in the class over to play, hoping Lauren would begin to make friends. But somehow the friendships never stuck. Her best friend was Meghan, our neighbour down the street. Meghan was a year older and so not in Lauren's class. They played together after school and on the weekends, but never socialized during school hours. Apparently it is one of the unwritten rules on the school playground: Never hang out with anyone either older or younger than you are. It just isn't cool.

Apart from the social stress of not having many friends, Lauren often found school boring. One afternoon she came home and announced angrily that her teacher said they had to study dinosaurs. "I don't care about dinosaurs. I want to know about horses," said Lauren insistently. The next day, when I asked Mrs. Morris, Lauren's teacher, whether Lauren could study horses instead of dinosaurs, she told me, "No. We can't have part of the class doing one thing, while some others are doing something different. We all have to learn together."

Lauren was constantly sick. When I look back at her grade one school picture I am shocked at the gaunt little face; it is a picture of a sick little girl. Her shoulder-length blonde hair hangs limply and her large green eyes seem sunken beneath their well-defined dark eyebrows. I recall that Lauren was recovering from bronchitis at the time the picture was taken, and had lost ten pounds. Every other week she seemed to have a new cold. She was irritable and volatile and prone to tantrums. On Sunday afternoons she often developed a stomach ache, and on Monday mornings it became harder and harder to persuade her to get ready for school. Once or twice — I hate to admit this — I physically dragged her from the back of her closet and forced her to get dressed.

Here is a journal entry from the fall of 1991.

> I had another horrible fight with Lauren about going to school. We took the morning off to go to the dentist. Then after lunch when I told Lauren it was time to go back to school the hysterics began. I don't know how to handle them. I tried coaxing, cuddling, sympathizing, remonstrating, threatening. Nothing worked. Finally Lauren ran upstairs

*and burrowed, sobbing, into my bed after I'd counted to ten
and then threatened to "ground" her and not let her watch
TV all week. I lost. I gave up and took Marlise to preschool
down the street. When I got back Lauren was fast asleep,
tear stains still on her cheeks. What do I do? I seem to be
the only one I know whose kid is so stressed out by school.
Why? How can I help her? I think I'm too hard on her, but
I can't just let her stay home. She has such a powerful little
will. She's so stubborn and intense in her feelings, it's almost
impossible to coax her when she's unwilling.*

We struggled through grade one and the first half of grade
two. Lauren's anger and frustration were more and more
evident with each passing week. She wasn't only resistant to going to
school, she was irritable and disruptive at home. The smallest
things seemed to frustrate her, often resulting in angry outbursts.
At times she would even lash out, either physically or with cruel
words, at Marlise or Julia.

I didn't know how to handle Lauren's tantrums and I had no
experienced friends whose parenting style I'd admired to advise
me. Relatives and neighbours persuaded me that I should gain
control of the situation by giving Lauren "time-outs" when she
"misbehaved." Once, in desperation, I even hauled my screaming
daughter into a cold shower! I shudder with shame to remember
this low point in our relationship. Needless to say, punishing
Lauren for her negative feelings only made the situation worse.
And treating her so cruelly made me feel like a monster rather
than a loving human being.

In late spring I began to panic. I made an appointment with
the school counselor. One Friday morning I dropped Marlise off at
a friend's and arrived at the school office with Julia in a backpack.
The counselor was a woman in her fifties, with crisp hair and
red fingernails. She glanced condescendingly at the baby on my
back, seeming to count it against me that I had not arranged a
sitter. I explained why I had come. She nodded knowingly. Then,
in a smooth and measured voice, she explained to me that Lauren

had "school phobia." My daughter was "too attached to me." The solution, she asserted, was for me to accompany Lauren to the classroom each day and calmly but emphatically insist that she go through the door alone. I was not to go in with her or hang around. I should make a "clear separation between school and home." It was all for the best, she reassured me. Lauren would outgrow her phobia in good time and begin to "fit in" with the other children.

I went away from the meeting feeling a mixture of anger and humiliation. What did this woman — this total stranger — know about my daughter? How dare she judge me as a poor parent and imply that Lauren's attachment to me was abnormal? Seven-year-olds were supposed to be attached to their mothers, weren't they? *Was* my daughter disabled? *Was* she too attached? I felt miserable and confused. It was recess. The school playground, as I passed through, was filled with apparently happy, noisy kids running and screaming in every direction. None of them seemed to have "school phobia." What was wrong with Lauren?

I stewed for several days and had just about made up my mind to try the tough love approach advocated by the school counselor, when the elementary school teachers in our city decided to go on strike. The strike was going to last for at least a week, they said. Whew! I thought, a vacation from the whole problem of school.

Lauren was ecstatic. It was May and the days were already long and warm. I took Marlise out of preschool and the three girls and I spent luxurious days at the park or on the beach or walking in the woods. A week passed and the strike continued. Another week passed. Lauren began to relax. She was like her old self again, open and responsive, full of energy and enthusiasm and creativity, and eager to enjoy the company of her sisters. I realized how much I'd missed her all winter — missed that bright and cheerful little girl who had become buried under anxiety. Richard noticed too. The strike went on. Other parents on my street were furious. They resented the inconvenience of finding childcare during the day. Furthermore, they worried that their children were "falling behind" schedule and would never be able to catch up. I listened to their fears politely, without comment. I was having too much fun playing hooky in the park with my kids to complain about the way things were going.

After nearly a month, the teachers negotiated a new contract and school reopened. It was the first day of June. I looked into Lauren's face and decided not to send her back. It's just one more month before summer holidays, I reasoned. What is the point of trying to get her re-adapted to school for such a short time? Richard backed my decision. Lauren would be a different child by next September — a whole three months older. She would be ready to return to school then.

Summer went by too fast. As September approached I began to feel a heaviness in my chest. I dreaded having to resume the old battle. I knew that Lauren wouldn't want to go back to school. She'd been so happy all summer. She had gained weight and seemed healthy and strong for the first time in a year. What was I going to do? A friend recommended I read a book on "spirited children." She told me Lauren was especially strong-willed and perhaps needed special handling. All right, I thought, I'll do some research. Maybe there's a book somewhere that will tell me how to help Lauren adjust to school.

One Saturday in late August I left the kids with Richard and made a trip to the bookstore. I stood for what seemed like hours in front of the Parenting section, leafing through books on all sorts of "syndromes" that could beset children, from Hyperactivity Disorder to Antisocial Behaviour Disorder to Attention Deficit Disorder. Wow, I thought, it is sure hard to raise an ordinary healthy kid these days. How could they all be so messed up? I didn't know what I was looking for and to this day I don't know why my feet led me past Parenting to the Education section. I stooped to the lowest shelf, where a book with a bright blue cover caught my eye for some reason. The author's name was vaguely familiar. John Holt. The book was called *Teach Your Own*.

A sudden current of electricity ran through me. I straightened, glancing guiltily over my shoulder as if what I clutched in my hands was not a mere book but something forbidden, dangerous, contraband. *Teach Your Own*. What subversive words. I felt scared of where they might lead me. Put the book back, a small voice inside said. That's not the book you want!

Sometimes when we look back on our lives, we realize that at a specific moment, on a certain ordinary morning or afternoon while we were going about the random business of our lives, the future happened. History notes a demarcation point, creating ever afterwards a "before and after." This sudden change in direction might result from a chance encounter with a stranger, or from a snatch of overheard conversation, or from a wrong turn while driving that leads to some unexpected discovery. The significance of the event might go unnoticed for days or years. But eventually you know: On that day it happened. That moment was the beginning of the rest of your life.

For me it was picking up a book. I bought *Teach Your Own* and skulked home with it like a criminal. I read it voraciously and furtively in a few days, then read it again. I'd never before in my life felt so moved and disturbed by a book. I felt like everything I read was addressed to me personally; everything was pointing, urging, calling to me. And I felt extremely scared. Ever since adolescence I'd had an irrational fear of being conspicuous. I tended to avoid conflict and I hated to stand out in a crowd. I wasn't a hippy or a flamboyant dresser or an outspoken social activist or anything that would cause people to notice me. I think I suffered from a type of performance anxiety left over from my high school years (a period when I felt that if I stuck out in any way I would attract either scorn or envy). What this book was inviting me to do was to become nothing less than an exhibitionist! Take my children out of school? Everyone would notice. I'd be questioned and judged. I'd become the topic of neighbourhood gossip. People would think I was eccentric. Or worse, plain nuts.

I remembered where I'd heard the author's name before. It was at the park, long ago. That homeschooling mother — whom I'd pitied at the time as odd and misguided — had mentioned

John Holt. His writing must have had a similar effect on her. As I read Holt's stories of families who had removed their children from school and allowed them to learn at their own pace and in their own way, my whole being said YES! Lauren's dislike of school was not a sign of disability or failure, but an indication that something strong and beautiful in her little soul was very alive and well. The school counselor had insinuated that Lauren had a "problem." But what if school itself was the problem? What if, rather than trying to "fix" Lauren, we just simply quit?

The notion was breathtaking. And terrifying. I tried it out on Richard and he panicked. She'll never have any friends, he said. She'll miss out on all the good stuff that comes with school — the team sports and school plays and recess hopscotch. She'll be lonely and bored at home. She'll end up psychologically gimped!

My mother was no better. When I called to discuss the idea on the phone with her she said, "If you don't send her to school she'll never differentiate from you. She'll stay dependent, glued to you for life." Why was this idea such a hard sell, I wondered? How had the idea of schooling become so sacrosanct, so impossible to question? I felt as if I were proposing to sell my children's souls to the devil. School seemed to have replaced good old-fashioned religion as the one thing that could rescue a child from depravity.

"Just for a year," I explained. "A year can't hurt." I was adamant. When I look back on the intensity of my commitment to the decision to take Lauren out of school, I realize that more was at stake than just her happiness. Something was calling to *me* as well. I sensed a door opening onto a new way of being in the world, a way far from the competitive, consumerist values of my culture.

Joseph Campbell, who studied the world's myths and found in them powerful insights into our common human experience, wrote a great deal about the "adventure of the Hero." We are all, he felt, summoned by Life to embark on a heroic journey towards self-realization. In a lecture he gave at the Esalen Institute in 1983, he described the call to adventure this way:

The call is to leave a certain social situation, move into your own loneliness and find the jewel, the center that's impossible to find when you're socially engaged. You are thrown off-center, and when you feel off-center, it's time to go. This is the departure when the hero feels something has been lost and goes to find it. You are to cross the threshold into new life. It's a dangerous adventure, because you are moving out of the sphere of the knowledge of you and your community. [4]

I had felt for years that I somehow didn't fit into my culture. Why did I so much want to be with my young children rather than "fulfill my potential" in some professional setting? Was I lazy? Irresponsible? Why couldn't I, as one friend called it, "get with the program"?

It seemed unfair to make Richard earn all the money. But I also knew he didn't want to be an at-home dad. He was passionate about being an architect and wanted to put all his best time and energy into the pursuit of his career. I think now we should have discussed more clearly with each other exactly what was at stake. We could have made some *conscious* decisions about the kind of family life we wanted to create, and how to divide the task of running a home. But we were young and overwhelmed and still not fully aware ourselves of what we wanted from life.

Though I felt guilty about my lack of career ambition, I was stubborn in my resistance to being pushed into a way of life I couldn't believe in. Why did the goals of my culture seem so empty to me? I had no answers, only self-doubt and discomfort. According to Campbell, discomfort is often the first step. Feeling at odds with one's world is often a sign of having crossed the threshold and commenced the hero's quest. He puts it this way:

When you cross the threshold, you are entering into the dark forest, taking a plunge into the sea, embarking on the night sea journey. It involves passing through clashing rocks, narrow gates and the like, which represent yes and no, the pairs of opposites . . . What this represents psychologically is the trip from the realm of conscious, rational intentions into the zone of those energies of the body that are moving from another center: the center with which you are trying to get in touch. [5]

I didn't know at the time what was missing, but I was aware that it had something to do with what Campbell refers to as "the energies of the body." It had to do with life-force, with power, or what the Chinese call "Qi" (pronounced "chee"). I wasn't in touch with my own Qi. Something in me lay unaddressed and unawakened. Perhaps it was not until I saw how my seven-year-old daughter after three years of school was beginning to lose touch with *her* powerful, exuberant life-force, that I realized how far I'd strayed from my own. After all, I had been thoroughly schooled. I had been a "good" student right through from kindergarten to graduate school, always anxious to win the approval of those in charge. I had felt cramped and constrained by the constant subtle competition for academic success and popularity that underlies every school system no matter how progressive.

Lauren was not the only one who needed rescuing. We both needed to set out on the heroic adventure to rediscover the "jewel" of our own creative vitality. Perhaps that is why the choice to pull Lauren out of school felt so profoundly exciting and scary for me: I knew that it was going to be *my* journey as much as hers.

Chapter Two
Questioning the Paradigm

The beginning of love is to let those we love be perfectly themselves, and not to twist them to fit our own image. Otherwise we love only the reflection of ourselves we find in them. [6]

Thomas Merton

When I look back on those first months of officially "home schooling," I can't help shuddering. I hadn't yet questioned the basic assumption of school: that learning is the result of teaching. My motivation for letting Lauren stay home was to allow her to learn in a more relaxed, less stressful environment. But I still assumed she would have to learn all the same things her schooled peers were learning. It was now my duty, I felt, to make sure she and her sisters didn't "fall behind."

We didn't have a special school room set up in our house, but that September I tried to convert our dining room into a classroom for at least a few hours each day. I bought a set of what I thought were inviting-looking workbooks on math and spelling for Lauren and Marlise, pens and pencils and pencil crayons, and lots of fresh white paper. I researched the official "learning outcomes" for their grade level recommended in the teachers' handbook issued by our provincial government. I intended to make sure the girls spent at least some time each day "on task" and that they covered all the aspects of the school curriculum.

I was excited and eager to get started. Learning at home was going to be fun!

It was not. It was hell. Lauren seemed keen at first. Probably because she was so relieved to be allowed to stay home from school, she tried as hard as she could to humour me. She arrived at the table the first morning eager to do the exercises I assigned her. After a few days, however, I noticed signs of discomfort. She didn't enjoy the spelling. She found the math difficult. She would doodle in her workbook or stare out the window rather than answer the questions I cheerfully gave her. Her body language told the tale most clearly: slumped in her chair with hunched shoulders and a furrowed brow, she looked like someone braced for attack rather than a child delighted to be learning new things.

I kept pushing, hoping she would adapt to the new routine. But another week passed and Lauren had had enough. One morning she burst into tears and threw her workbook across the room. "I *hate* this stuff!" she shouted. Then she stomped up to her bedroom and slammed the door. Marlise, who'd been having fun playing "school" since she was only in kindergarten and didn't yet have to tackle anything frustrating like arithmetic, got up from the table and glowered at me. "I'm going to go play with Lauren," she said, ever loyal to her older sister. "I don't like school either!"

Julia had been happily singing to her stuffed animals on the couch in the living room. When she heard the workbook smash against the wall, she looked up startled. She must have sensed my unhappiness because she immediately got to her feet. She retrieved the tossed workbook and offered it to me with a sympathetic expression on her two-year-old face. I thanked her, then sat at the empty table and absently fingered the reviled workbook. What was I going to do? I just couldn't bring myself to enforce "school time" each day against the girls' will by using threats or punishments. How could I make them *want* to do the assignments?

I decided to try bribery. The next day I sat the girls down and made a deal: "I'll let you buy that new Playmobile farm set you've been wanting once you both finish your workbooks." Lauren's was a grade three math book, and Marlise's was a beginning spelling workbook that was mostly pictures. Lauren and Marlise agreed. They'd been desperate for the set of pasture fences and the palomino pony that came with this miniature toy set. Lauren returned to the table, gritted her teeth and slogged through the arithmetic workbook in only three days. I was a bit dismayed. I should have made a better bargain. I should have required more work for such a big prize. I thought it would take her weeks to get through that workbook!

Next negotiating session I raised the stakes and asked for more effort: two workbooks this time, a math *and* a spelling, and they'd get the Black Stallion set. I felt like one of those desperate gamblers unable to stop placing bets despite a sinking feeling my luck was running out. None of this felt right. Rewarding the girls for doing what was obviously unpleasant felt abusive. What did the prize have to do with the task that won it? Shouldn't children learn about the world because they are *curious* about how it works? Didn't I want them to grow up able to set their own goals and pursue their own interests and passions? This bribery business seemed more about training them, like dogs, to do tricks for a biscuit.

Even though she wanted the rewards, Lauren's hunched and resistant attitude to learning remained. In fact, the rewards seemed to be making the problem worse. The expression on her face was more closed and defensive than ever. She was angry, just as she had been during the previous winter at school. Gone was the relationship we'd enjoyed all summer of trusting, relaxed spontaneity. I had a permanent knot in my stomach. We were both miserable.

Several times the thought crossed my mind that sending Lauren back to school would be so much easier than these constant negotiations and battles. At least at school her frustration at being bullied and controlled would be directed against her teacher and not against me. At school she would do what she was told because she would be too scared not to. I could go back to being the nice safe mommy who had milk and cookies and hugs ready for her when she got home from a difficult day. But I didn't want Lauren to spend her days either angry or afraid. And I knew I couldn't go on bribing her to obey me. Trying to control her felt deeply, fundamentally wrong.

I kept reading every book on alternative approaches to education I could get my hands on, hoping to find some helpful advice. At last I stumbled upon the writings of American writer and scholar Alfie Kohn. In his book, *Punished by Rewards: The Trouble with Gold Stars, Incentive Plans, A's, Praise, and Other Bribes*, Kohn reviews the findings of several hundred scientific investigations of human motivation and concludes that all people, including children, become less likely in the long run to engage in a given activity if they have been either punished or rewarded for doing so. He distinguishes between "intrinsic" and "extrinsic" motivation.[7] Being intrinsically motivated to do a given task means that we do it because it is deeply satisfying. The activity is its own reward. When we are extrinsically motivated, we do the work not because it is satisfying or meaningful in itself but because by doing so we will either avoid a painful consequence or win some kind of treat such as praise or a benefit or prize.

The problem with "extrinsic motivators," argues Kohn, is that "a child promised a treat for learning or acting responsibly has been given every reason to stop doing so when there is no longer a reward to be gained."[8] Children who are told "read these books and I will buy that bicycle you want so badly" are not helped to discover the intrinsic joys of reading, for instance. They are more likely to suspect that reading is, in fact, a boring and unpleasant chore. Otherwise, why the bribe?

Nor is the child who is rewarded for being "nice" to other children helped to become a nicer person. According to one study cited by Kohn, "children who were frequently praised for displays of generosity tended to be slightly less generous on an everyday basis than other children were. Every time they had heard 'Good sharing!' or 'I'm so proud of you for helping,' they became a little less interested in sharing or helping. Those actions came to be seen not as something valuable in their own right but as something they had to do to get that reaction again from an adult. Generosity became a means to an end."[9]

Alfie Kohn's research corroborated my own first-hand experience with my daughters: rewarding children is as much a form of coercion as is punishing them. Both punishing and rewarding feel *wrong*, because both are acts of dominance and control. Both are profoundly disrespectful. Moreover, neither rewards nor punishments work as motivating tools because they don't allow human beings to develop their own reasons for doing things. We might succeed for a while in getting our child to perform a task in exchange for a prize. In the long run, however, we are going to have a real problem on our hands. Whatever we "pay" kids for doing, whether we reward them with praise, good grades, toys or money, becomes unappealing once the payments stop.

I agreed with Kohn that extrinsic motivation just isn't sustainable in the long run. Furthermore, I was beginning to sense that something tragic happens to relationships when people attempt to control each other. When parents or employers or heads of state force others to obey them by using either punishments or rewards, the quality of human connection erodes. When we allow systems of hierarchy and coercion to shape the world, we end up losing what matters most. We lose each other.

I have felt uneasy with competition from day one. But growing up in a culture founded on labelling, judging and ranking made me doubt my instincts. As a child I was bombarded with the ethic of win/lose. Everywhere — at school, on the sports field, in the media — I saw competition extolled as not only healthy but essential to a successful society. I sensed early on that the job of our cultural institutions seems to be to sort winners from losers, to select the few who get to be in charge. Those who don't make it to the top are supposed to be "good sports" and put up with life as a zero-sum game.

This emphasis on winning and losing was painful for me as a child. From a very early age I had a fierce sense of justice, and was intensely aware of the moods and attitudes of others. I wanted everyone to be treated kindly and fairly and was outraged at the spectacle of bullying. Even though I loved sports, I felt just as uncomfortable winning the race as losing. I didn't like it when teachers selected one child for praise and another for disapproval, even when that praised child happened to be me.

At times I have wondered whether my reactions were neurotic. Many of my adult friends, whom I respect and know to be thoughtful and well-intentioned, don't seem disturbed to their very roots by the idea of coercing children (through the use of either rewards or punishments) to behave in ways they consider "good." How can they be sure, I have often wondered, that the end they are trying to achieve is worth such unkind means? I still remember vividly what it was like to be a child. When a teacher or relative shamed or scolded me, or said "Just do as I say!" I felt violated. When an adult patted me on the head and said "Good girl!" I felt manipulated and patronized. Did my friends have an entirely different experience as youngsters? Was my extreme sensitivity to imbalances of power in human relationships normal?

My parents treated me with respect at home. My father, Lee, and my mother, Lorita, were highly sensitive and gentle. They never undermined me or disregarded my feelings. Both had been raised in a Mormon culture. Both had, after painful struggle, renounced that culture and moved far away from their families. Their Mormon childhood left my parents with a deep distrust of authority. My father describes himself as an "existentialist," believing that, in the absence of any certain truth about the purpose of existence, each of us must take responsibility for our own choices. My mother, too, rejected her religion at an early age. In her thirties, however, she embraced a form of Hinduism and still practices daily meditation.

My parents tried hard not to repeat the patterns of their own upbringing. As far as I remember, I was rarely punished. Instead, they always took the time to explain their decisions as clearly to me as they could, and left me free to make my own choices wherever possible. But on the school playground, or in the homes of my friends, I was often shocked to witness adults or older children behaving in domineering ways to those younger or less powerful. Such ways of relating seemed to me deeply wrong.

My parents sometimes found my strong sense of fairness embarrassing. My mother tells the story of my seventh birthday party. We'd invited some of the neighbourhood children over, as well as all the girls in my class at school. I was the queen of the day, and evidently enjoyed the limelight. We played party games like Pin the Tail on the Donkey, tag and hide and seek. All was going well until Peter, the boy across the lane I played with every weekend, decided to tease a girl from my class. Leila was overweight and unable to run fast. When she got out of breath and dropped out of the game of tag, Peter started shouting "Fatso! Fatso! Put her in a vat-so!" Leila, used to abuse, just shrugged. But I, apparently, was furious. I stormed over to him and said, "You're mean! Go home right now!" I grabbed his t-shirt and marched him to the back gate, shoved him through and slammed it shut. Peter didn't get any birthday cake or party favours. His mother was quite upset at the brutal way he'd been expelled from the party, and complained loudly to my mom the next day. But I refused to apologize.

My native hypersensitivity was made even more intense by the traumatic experience of my parents' divorce when I was ten years old. My mother's twin brother had committed suicide the year before, at the age of thirty. For months following his death, Mom spent hours walking alone for miles, plunged into confusion and despair. Her own unresolved childhood pain, the legacy of a narcissistic and rejecting mother, surfaced. She felt trapped in a life she wasn't fully choosing. She realized that had married far too young — at the age of nineteen, before she'd had a chance to live on her own, or finish college, or even learn to drive. Even though she cared a great deal about my father, she decided she had to leave the marriage in order to discover how to rely on herself. In a way, her twin brother's suicide was for my mother a kind of ultimatum: either embrace life fully, or give up and follow him into death.

Mom moved out. My brother, Paul, and I continued to live with my father in the house that had been our family home before the divorce. Several years later, Dad remarried and my stepmother, Pegeen, who like my dad was an English professor at the University of British Columbia, came to live with us. But until then, Mom came by every evening to read to us and put us to bed. I imagine the arrangement must have been emotionally very difficult for my parents, but I am very grateful to them for their generosity. Having my mother there every evening made the crisis a lot easier to bear.

Although my parents tried hard to reassure us that the breakup was not our fault, my brother and I suffered. What was traumatic for me, as a very empathetic child, was to see how sad my father was, and how ashamed and guilt-ridden my mother was, at the time of their breakup. I became suddenly and painfully aware that life was difficult and risky, that nothing was "safe" or guaranteed to last. I wanted more than anything to make them feel better somehow. My response was to suppress my own needs and be "good" so that they wouldn't have to worry about me too.

Many of us were wounded as children. Life is fraught with change, loss and disappointment, no matter how materially advantaged we are. But perhaps we react to our trauma in different ways. My early sense of the sadness and difficulty of life intensified my natural desire to protect others. I wanted to save others from suffering, to shield them from criticism or blame. I wanted to help "fix" what was not working in their lives, and this desire sometimes came at the expense of my own needs. As a teenager and young woman I often felt that there was no impermeable layer or boundary separating me from other people. The reality of others flooded through me. I didn't know how to protect myself. There were periods when I hesitated to go to a party or talk to someone new, because I felt unable to "take someone else on." Merely to talk to another person was to see them too intimately for my own safety and comfort. I felt invaded by what I perceived as their feelings and needs, especially by any pain I sensed in them.

My challenge over the years has been to learn to live with my capacity for empathy in ways that don't drain or harm me. I have had to train myself to resist taking on the suffering of others at the expense of my own well-being.

Even with this strong empathy, however, I have also always been keenly aware of others as *other*, as souls with their own sacred reality. I now realize that this awareness is not neurotic but is, in fact, the very basis for compassion. My compassionate awareness of my children was what was creating such a problem for me all those years ago, as I struggled to "teach" them at home. I sensed, even before I could articulate it, that in any relationship between two people, when one sits in judgment over the other and is able, therefore, to dispense or withhold approval, one holds all the power. It is not a relationship of equals. Those who await judgment do not feel safe or relaxed or unconditionally loved. Instead, they walk on eggshells. In order to feel safe, they are obliged to win the favour of the person in charge.

In the futuristic movie *Avatar*, the indigenous inhabitants of Pandora greet each other with the phrase "I see you." They model what happens when you "see" others, whether in human or non-human form, not as things but as luminous presences sharing your world. You cannot view them as means to an end. You cannot use them to get something that you want. Any thought of compelling or manipulating another to do your bidding becomes inconceivable once you open your eyes and heart to their full, separate reality. Others are not objects like chairs or tools, to be used or acted upon. Instead, they are mysterious worlds unto themselves, sources of meaning and agency that can only be encountered, never exploited.

Such seeing is, I believe, a prerequisite for love. Relationship means the connection between two separate entities. When we fail to see others as *other*, we can relate only to ourselves. In the words of Thomas Merton, when we "twist" others so that they "fit our own image" of what is right or good, we end up seeing only "the reflection of ourselves we find in them." We end up alone.

My moral crisis that first year I took my children out of school was that I could not cease to see them as sacred others and yet I felt required by my culture to do exactly that. I wanted to look into my seven-year-old daughter's eyes and say, "I see you." And I wanted her to look back at me with the same open and loving gaze. I had a powerful intuition that anything less would mean the loss of the precious intimacy between us. It would be like going blind.

Chapter Three
The Paradigm Shifts

If the emotions are free the intellect will look after itself. [10]

A.S. Neill

One morning during this stressful period, after another fight with Lauren over schoolwork, I sat with a cup of coffee at the kitchen table and watched Julia playing. She had opened one of the kitchen doors and was pulling out various bowls and utensils. For a few minutes she explored the noises they made when banged together. Then she took hold of two plastic Tupperware containers and two plastic lids. The square containers were approximately the same size and so were the lids. But they were subtly different in shape. One was exactly square while the other had slightly rounded corners. Julia tried to fit one of the plastic lids to one of the containers. She pushed and pushed, but it wouldn't snap down. She tried the other container and lid, still with no success. With a furrowed brow, she turned the two lids over in her hands. The problem obviously puzzled her. Why couldn't she fit the lids on the containers the way she had seen Mommy do it earlier that morning?

Julia examined the objects carefully for a moment. Then she tried switching the lids. The square lid snapped down neatly on the square container! Julia's eyes widened with satisfaction.

She tried the other lid and it fit too. Immediately, she got to her feet and proudly brought me the objects. "Lookit!" she said. I looked and admired. "You do it!" she commanded. Obediently, I snapped off the lids, then reassembled them while Julia watched with eager interest. Satisfied that we had shared this wonderful discovery, she took the containers — each with its tight-fitting lid now firmly in place — from my hands. She put them back in the drawer. Then, forgetting all about her recent adventure, she began to explore a set of measuring spoons.

We don't seem to worry much about whether toddlers are learning enough, I mused as I watched Julia play. We trust them to grow and learn every day without formal lessons or coaching. Young children are determined investigators of the world. A one-year-old has no fear of failure! If she wants to toddle across the room, or climb on a chair, or open a box, or learn to pronounce the cat's name, she will persist in her attempts without embarrassment or fear. She will try, try and try again, despite falls and frustrations of every sort, until she finally masters whatever skill seems so enticing at the time. She doesn't need "motivating." She just needs the companionship of someone she trusts to sit nearby while she explores, someone who is ready to celebrate her discoveries when she makes them.

It was so much easier to trust young children, I thought, and to accept the natural differences in their developmental timetables. One child learns to walk at ten months and talk fluently at two, for instance, while another walks at eighteen months and doesn't say much until three years old. Once children reach school age, why does it suddenly become so much more difficult to have faith in them? When did we persuade ourselves that older children can't carry on as they began, but instead have to be forced to learn, all together, at the same rate and at the same time?

John Taylor Gatto is a historian, a former schoolteacher and an outspoken critic of modern schooling who has twice won the New York State teacher of the year award. In *Dumbing Us Down* and *Weapons of Mass Instruction: A Schoolteacher's Journey through the Dark World of Compulsory Schooling*, he explores the philosophical and cultural roots of what he calls "compulsion schooling."[11] He points out that underlying our model of "public education" are two sinister world views: that human nature is mechanistic and quantifiable, and that human society is by nature hierarchical, with the few entitled to rule over the many.

The mechanistic world view that fueled the industrial revolution saw individual people as cogs in a giant machine: society should function like a well-oiled clock or a productive factory. The first modern schools, Gatto points out, were in fact deliberately modeled on factories. They were designed to be like assembly lines, where raw human material (in the form of children) could be transformed into skilled, compliant workers for the expanding economy.

Gatto chillingly quotes directly from historic speeches and texts by various "founding fathers" of modern schooling. President Woodrow Wilson, in a speech to a gathering of New York businessmen in 1909, summed up the purpose of public schooling in a few choice words. "We want one class to have a liberal education. We want another class, a very much larger class of necessity, to forgo the privilege of a liberal education and fit themselves to perform specific difficult manual tasks."[12] The 1906 "mission statement" of Vice President John D. Rockefeller's General Education Board states even more clearly that the aim of public schooling (as opposed to private) was to create a "perfect," obedient workforce:

In our dreams . . . people yield themselves with perfect docility to our molding hands . . . Unhampered by tradition we work our own good will upon a grateful and responsive folk. We shall not try to make these people or any of their children into philosophers or men of learning or men of science. We have not to raise up from among them authors, educators, poets or men of letters. We shall not search for embryo great artists, painters, musicians, nor lawyers, doctors, preachers, politicians, statesmen, of whom we have ample supply. The task we set before ourselves is very simple . . . we will organize children . . . and teach them to do in a perfect way the things their fathers and mothers are doing in an imperfect way.[13]

This statement, written by the rich and powerful shapers of American society at the turn of the last century, sends shivers down my spine. What a flagrant exaltation of power! These men never for a moment intended to send their own children to be "molded" by public schools. No — *their* children would be educated privately, groomed for positions of power, in expensive, specialized schools or by tutors. Their children would not be required to learn by rote, like sheep, but would be encouraged to think critically and creatively. The expanding industrial empire couldn't afford to have too many independent thinkers. Instead, the fathers of public education knew that to keep the wheels of industry turning — and their profits growing — a constant supply of willing workers and civil servants was crucial. They designed schools that would prepare children for a lifetime of deferring to the judgment of a privileged and powerful few. Most importantly, they kept this intent a secret by advertising schools as agents of democracy and opportunity.

The frightening truth is that schooling *works*. In Gatto's words, "who besides a degraded rabble would voluntarily present itself to be graded and classified like meat?" Well-trained children grow up to be responsive to the commands of those in authority. They learn not to trust their own judgment and intelligence, and so don't tend to challenge the status quo. They buy what's advertised on TV, believe without question what's shown on the news and go willingly to war when their leaders command it. Schools teach children to let others decide what matters.

Wendy Priesnitz, publisher of *Life Learning Magazine* and *Natural Life Magazine*, and author of many books on alternative education, links the way we treat children to the way we treat the natural world. "Public education," she writes, "reflects our society's paternalistic, hierarchical world view, which exploits children in the same way it takes the earth's resources for granted."[14] The objectifying gaze that reduces children to lumps of raw material to be "standardized" also sees the complex, interdependent web of life on earth as a sum of "resources" to be extracted. When we do not see others, we become capable of violence towards them. It is easy to brutalize those we do not radically respect, whether they are children or forests.

When I first read their views, I wanted to believe that Gatto's and Priesnitz's positions are too extreme. Times have changed, haven't they? We have come a long way since the early days of public schooling, and most educators today have a more humane and holistic approach to education than they did in 1906. We no longer cane children for misbehaving or make them sit in corners wearing dunce hats. In theory at least, educators value the "whole child" and acknowledge that there are many ways for children to learn. Special programs try to meet the needs of disadvantaged or disabled students. Art and music programs (where they haven't been eliminated by funding cutbacks) aim to cultivate children's creativity.

But when I remembered walking through the halls of Lauren's school, I realized that the old paradigm is still alive and well. Within individual classrooms there are indeed many good-hearted teachers treating their students with respect. The *structure* of school itself, however, teaches another lesson. In the end, the medium is the message: the long, shiny corridors, the age-segregated classrooms, the fenced play yards, the separate staff room and principal's office, the compulsory attendance, the ringing bells, the late slips, the grades, report cards and standardized testing, still tell that same old story of factory-style mass production. As Priesnitz so aptly says, "one of our most revered and supposedly democratic institutions uses the tool of compulsion to subject children to a standardized curriculum, molds them into obedient consumers and fits them into their places in the hierarchy."[15]

I knew one thing for sure: living creatures are not machine parts that can be mass-produced. There has never been, and never will be, anything standard about children. They are too intelligent, too complex, too idiosyncratic. They won't all willingly or joyfully learn the same things at the same time, ever, under any circumstances, no matter how many tricks the adults around them employ. Some will want to find out about dinosaurs while others are keen on horses. Some won't be curious about any creature on the good green earth. At least not right now. The possible areas of interest a human mind might find fascinating are nearly infinite. What curriculum could ever claim to include them all? There isn't one, nor ever will be.

Nope. The whole notion of school had to go.

Once I rejected the implicit assumption that *children must be made to learn what the adults in charge think they should know*, I knew we were going to be on our own. Our family would have to forge our own path. There would now be no manual, no map or waymarks to follow, no "learning outcomes" to point the way. The only guide would be our commitment to treat each other with mutual respect.

So what would our lives be like, now that we wouldn't be "schooling at home"? I returned to John Holt's book, *Teach Your Own*. Holt refers to learning without formal teaching as "unschooling," and distinguishes it from the approach of "homeschoolers." Homeschoolers, he says, reject school for various reasons, often religious ones, but do not necessarily reject either the notion that all children should learn certain things at certain ages or that coercion is an appropriate educational tool. Unschoolers, in contrast, want to "grow without schooling." Other writers since Holt have called this non-coercive approach "de-schooling," "natural-learning" and "life-learning."

The unschooling approach to learning that Holt describes reflects, for me, the true meaning of the word "education." The term derives from the Latin *educere*, meaning "to bring out, to lead forth." Unlike the social engineering vision of Gatto's industrialists, education is not a process of moulding a child to fit the needs and demands of others. Instead, an educator's role is to bring forth and allow to flourish *what is already present* in the child. An education allows the child to blossom into his own fullness. It sets him on his unique path into the heart of life.

In *Teach Your Own*, Holt shows how a true education puts the learner in charge of his or her learning. It occurs in an environment of mutual trust and respect, free of coercion or domination, and requires what all the families portrayed in Holt's book share: a powerful faith in the natural processes of life. The unschooling families Holt describes believe that children — indeed, people of all ages — naturally seek to grow and explore and connect with the world around us. Human beings don't need to be taught how to learn; learning is what we do best, and do all the time.

I found Holt's many interviews with unschoolers very inspiring. These families allow their children to learn from life in a natural, unhurried, organic way, without the outside pressure of timetables, fixed curricula, tests or grades. Some of these families live in rural areas, on farms or in cabins in the woods. Their children work alongside them, helping to grow food or build shelters or repair farm machinery when they are not riding horses or playing a musical instrument. Other families live in cities and spend time visiting libraries or museums or volunteering for local charities. The important thing, for Holt, is that there is no right way for children and parents to live and learn together. The lifestyles of the unschoolers he describes are as varied as the people who live them. And as people grow and change, interests change too. Education is an unfolding process that often takes surprising twists and turns.

Reading Holt's book helped me realize that there were other parents in the world who felt as I did. I set about trying to meet some of them. The girls and I began to attend some of the Vancouver Homelearners' Association's daytime activities. Richard joined us for monthly evening gatherings. Many of the parents we met at these gatherings had made big sacrifices in order to keep their kids at home. Many seemed to have mastered the art of living gracefully on little money. These families made things by hand, grew big gardens and shopped at thrift stores. They cut costs wherever they could so that they could survive either on one salary, or on two part-time salaries. There was a single mom who worked from home. There were several at-home dads, whose partners brought home the paycheque. There was a couple who ran a home-based business that their two children helped to operate.

It was wonderful to meet other parents who treated their children with respect. These children, many of whom were older than mine, seemed bright and curious and engaged. I was surprised to find them speaking directly to me, in a relaxed, friendly way as if I were a peer, unlike the neighbourhood kids on our street who often seemed wary of adults.

These kids were used to being taken seriously. They were accustomed to being respected for their thoughts and opinions and often contributed to the conversations going on around them. Also, each seemed to have her or his own particular interests. One nine-year-old was a keen member of a performing circus troupe, an eleven-year-old loved to solve math puzzles and to play the violin, another was creating an elaborate graphic novel about a fantasy world he'd invented. The children were eager to tell me about their passions. Both their enthusiasm and their trust that I would take them seriously and not try to dominate or "teach" them shone from their eyes and softened their expressions. There were no hunched shoulders or sullen, resentful faces in this bunch.

The companionship of these other families helped me find the courage to keep walking the road less travelled. I surrendered control and decided to trust life. I let the children *play*. I put the workbooks away on a shelf where they could be retrieved if the kids so desired (they rarely did). I got rid of the TV. I made sure we always had plenty of art supplies and library books (of the kids' choosing) handy. But other than that, I tried to stop planning how we would spend the day and we began to go with the flow of our energy and enthusiasms. On sunny days we headed for the forest or the beach. On rainy days we went to the library or visited the science museum or stayed home by a cozy fire, reading aloud or drawing. I let the girls play imagination games for hours if they wanted to. I was available to ponder with them whatever questions arose in the course of our explorations. I often learned just as much from our fascinating conversations as they did. The sullen resentment disappeared miraculously. Lauren seemed happy to spend time with me again.

Once I decided to trust my instincts, I felt a kind of power enter my body. Life came into sharp focus. I began to feel braver in social settings, and to speak up for my beliefs more often in conversations with others. I started to learn how to be "different" gracefully yet assertively. Ironically, when I gave up attempting to coerce my children, I myself became what Alfie Kohn would call more "intrinsically motivated." I became more able to make my own choices and decisions, without being compelled either by the desire to please others or by the fear of their disapproval.

The wonderful learning community we discovered in Vancouver was an invaluable support, especially in those early years. There were still times when periods of intense doubt would beset me. I needed the companionship of like-minded friends to keep my courage up. I needed to be able to trade ideas and resources with others. As a community we combined our talents and energies and finances in order to organize activities for our children. During our years in Vancouver my daughters participated in a variety of group activities: a "young Shakespeareans" acting troupe facilitated by professional actors, a creative writing club, a weekly "gym day" (where we had the use of a gymnasium and lots of sports equipment), a monthly "theme day" (when children and adults met in someone's home to share information on a chosen theme, from medieval times to dinosaurs to astronomy), a Dungeons and Dragons club, a monthly sing-along, an annual talent night, as well as many get-togethers at the park or beach to play with their unschooled friends.

The girls only participated when they wanted to. When one child was keen and another wasn't, we had to do some negotiating. There were times when one daughter would choose to sit apart with her nose in a book rather than participate in whatever the group was doing. But no one ever ridiculed or reproached her for doing so. Since the atmosphere at these gatherings was always easygoing and non-coercive, all three girls generally enjoyed them.

Chapter Four
The Language of Power

All the time you are in school, you learn through experience how to live in a dictatorship.[16]

Grace Llewellyn

When I began to trust my children to learn and grow according to their own inner rhythms, I watched my relationship with them become more relaxed, joyful and fun. I grieved for some of my friends and neighbours who seemed to be constantly locking horns with their children. One neighbour on my street had been advised by a counselor to try a "tough love" approach with her "willful" thirteen-year-old daughter. The approach wasn't working. The fights, tantrums, scoldings and punishments kept escalating. I watched mother and child grow more and more estranged from each other. It was heartbreaking.

I have observed that all people behave in destructive ways when they feel disempowered. When they feel pushed around and controlled, they either withdraw — punishing themselves by becoming depressed and anxious — or they get resentful and angry and try to hurt others. Children are no exception. When they feel dominated they behave badly, which often leads those in power (their parents and teachers) to try to exert even more control over them. Situations that allow some to dominate others bring out the worst both in the oppressor and the oppressed. Power can turn human beings into monsters.

Lauren had felt disempowered at school. First of all, she *had* to go. She couldn't just choose to stay home or to go somewhere else during the day. Secondly, once in school, she wasn't free to learn about what interested her. She was obliged to obey her teacher and perform whatever tasks were on the curriculum. She wasn't allowed to talk when she needed to, or to go outside to play when she felt restless. Also, she couldn't choose whom to spend her time with. She had to interact with the same children and the same teacher every day, whether she wanted to or not. (Mischa Sandberg, an unschooling dad, said once, "Imagine a group of adults forced to spend day after day cooped up together in a single room. Think of the lawsuits!") The daily dose of disempowerment had begun to transform Lauren into an angry, sulky, resentful and sickly child before my very eyes.

But it's not only in schools that children encounter the bullying of adults. I have a vivid (and painful) memory of an early confrontation with Lauren. She was about five years old and I'd hired a babysitter to look after her and Marlise while I went to visit a friend with Julia, who was still a baby. The babysitter, Jackie, was a woman in her fifties who had no children of her own. She took the girls to the park, and I guess at one point the wind came up and Jackie insisted that Lauren put on her coat. Lauren, who was always hot because she ran around so much, refused. Apparently she announced firmly, "I'm not wearing my coat, 'cause I'm not cold!" Jackie wouldn't take no for an answer. She grabbed Lauren and tried to force her into the coat. A battle ensued during which Lauren called Jackie a "stupid ass!" and then proceeded to run home from the park by herself.

I arrived back at the house to hear Jackie scolding Lauren loudly. Jackie was livid. Lauren had definitely managed to push all the woman's buttons! I asked what had happened and was treated to a tirade on what a badly behaved child I had. "She talks back! She has a dirty mouth!" Jackie asserted. "She's a very naughty child!"

I paid the babysitter and was relieved to see the last of her. Then I turned to Lauren, who was hunched on the couch with a bitter scowl on her little face. "What's wrong with you?" I began to reproach. "Why did you have to be so rude to Jackie? Why can't you cooperate and do what you're told?"

I stopped, shocked at hearing my own words. I looked at my daughter. She was very unhappy. She'd just had a really wretched experience. Someone had tried to force her to do something she was unwilling to do, and she was being humiliated and rebuked for standing up for herself. I hugged her tight and she burst into tears.

Why, just because someone is shorter than you, or less articulate, or less experienced, should they automatically have to bend to your will and "cooperate" with your wishes? Why does a paradigm of human relationship in which one person has power over another make sense to us at all? Even I, who prided myself on my respectful parenting, found myself ready to dominate my child in a stressful, unreflective moment. Old habits die hard.

A book that sheds wonderful light on the ways we use power is Marshall Rosenberg's *Nonviolent Communication: A Language of Life*. Rosenberg argues that the power-over paradigm is built into the very language we speak to one another. After centuries of living in what he calls "domination societies," we have grown used to engaging in "life-alienating communication."

> *Most of us grew up speaking a language that encourages us to label, compare, demand and pronounce judgments rather than to be aware of what we are feeling and needing. . . . Life-alienating communication both stems from and supports hierarchical or domination societies, where large populations are controlled by a small number of individuals to those individuals' own benefit. It would be in the interest of kings, czars, nobles and so forth that the masses be educated in a way that renders them slave-like in mentality. The language of wrongness, should and have to is perfectly suited for this purpose: the more people are*

trained to think in terms of moralistic judgments that imply wrongness and badness, the more they are being trained to look outside themselves — to outside authorities — for the definition of what constitutes right, wrong, good and bad. When we are in contact with our feelings and needs, we humans no longer make good slaves and underlings.[17]

Today, even though we no longer have kings and czars running things, we still seem to be quick to give away our power to "experts" who claim to know what's best for us. If John Taylor Gatto is right, schools have trained us to defer unquestioningly to those in positions of authority. We don't tend to challenge the right of presidents, CEOs, principals, professionals, newscasters, teachers, bosses, heads-of-families, doctors, PhDs and gurus to call the shots, because we assume they are "qualified" to be in charge. We are used to a hierarchical system in which not everyone gets an equal say.

I took an acting workshop once in which we played characters having various levels of social status. If we were high status, we held our heads up (literally with noses in the air), walked tall, stared directly into others' eyes and spoke with authority. If we were low status we dropped our heads, shuffled our feet, glanced furtively rather than directly and mumbled if we spoke at all. It was an enlightening experience. I discovered that it is deeply uncomfortable to inhabit the body of someone who feels disempowered. As a lowly person I felt tense and anxious and defensive. I also felt angry at those who lorded it over me. That day I understood in my bones how those at the bottom of the social ladder can become violent.

The workshop left me wondering. Is it just plain human nature to be so status conscious? Are humans *innately* hierarchical, like wolves or other pack animals? I was not convinced. Human nature is very complex. There must be many ways of being and relating that we haven't yet tried, many styles of social organization we have not explored. I suspect that hierarchical, status-driven societies are not "natural" or inevitable; they are just what we are used to. Our founding myths — at least those of the so-called great religions — have tended to represent a hierarchical world view: God at the top, then the priests and kings, then human beings, with the rest of the natural world at the bottom of the heap. Societies based on such a top-down model of reality can't help but be stratified; they do not celebrate all beings as sacred and worthy of equal respect, but instead enshrine a permanent cosmic pecking order.

Perhaps if we really want to change the ways in which we relate to one another, we have to recognize the "domination" stories at the root of our cultural paradigms. We need to create new stories that help us seek a world of mutual respect and reverence for all life.

The only way we can change the way we relate to each other is to first become conscious of our knee-jerk reactions and assumptions. Adults tend to treat children the way they themselves were once treated because they haven't reflected deeply on what is actually going on. Perhaps they have just plain forgotten how painful it was to be pushed around and bullied as a small child. Or perhaps they were so indoctrinated, when young, into the belief that their needs were less important than those of the adults around them that, many years later, they still carry this unquestioned belief buried deep in their hearts.

Lauren was the oldest of eight grandchildren on Richard's side. She had the tough job of teaching some of her older relatives to treat children more respectfully. Lauren's strong will and outspoken personality tended to trigger a strong reaction from adults who expected obedience from children. Lauren simply didn't buy into a hierarchical social paradigm in which she had no rights merely because she was a child. She wouldn't submit quietly to domination. Instead, she passionately and often eloquently pointed out inconsistencies and injustices in the behaviour of the adults around her.

When Lauren was eight years old, she had a confrontation with her grandfather that changed their relationship for the better. It was Easter and we were spending the holiday with my in-laws in their log cabin on Mayne Island. There were about five grandchildren there at the time, Lauren being the oldest, so it was very lively and noisy in the crowded cabin.

My father-in-law, Rand, enjoyed having his family around him. He was a tall, wiry man with a deep voice and a big personality. He liked being the centre of attention. He also enjoyed "teaching" his grandchildren. Though basically kind-hearted, he was used to being the boss. I had already had several run-ins with him when the children were smaller over his insistence that the girls be spanked for misbehaving (which I refused to do). Like my babysitter Jackie, he seemed to hold two powerful, but unexamined, assumptions when it came to handling children: that human nature is inherently selfish and that adults should be in charge. He thought it *made sense* to punish "bad" behaviour. Rand, like most of his generation, believed that undisciplined children would grow up to be brutes. Adults were duty-bound to train children to be good.

Normally the grandchildren would have been playing out of doors, but it was raining on this particular afternoon. After lunch, Rand decided to go upstairs for a nap, which turned out to be a bad idea, since there was almost no sound separation between the cabin's two floors. The kids, stuck inside, were full of beans. They began taking turns putting on "funny shows" for each other — a game in which one or two children would take the stage and improvise a comic skit for the others. Since the point was to make the others laugh, the game tended to get very loud.

After an unusually noisy burst of laughter and shrieking, we all heard a bellow from above. Rand stormed downstairs, his thin, white hair disheveled and his shirt half-untucked. He strode over to Lauren — who was sitting in a chair on the makeshift stage — bent over, and grasped her by the shoulders.

"Be quiet, dammit, or I'll turn you over my knee! Don't you know I'm trying to sleep? You kids are a bunch of hooligans!" Rand had a booming, bass voice. The younger children looked terrified.

Lauren gazed back at him steadily, her lip quivering. I rose from my seat. My mother-in-law and sister-in-law turned from where they had been washing dishes in the kitchen and watched anxiously. I felt shocked and outraged at how unfair and insensitive Rand was being. I wanted to intervene, but I kept my mouth shut.

Lauren shook herself free of her grandfather's grasp and glared at him. Then she stood up from her chair and said sternly, "Poppa! Sit down right here!"

Rand, surprised, sat down in her chair.

"Now listen to this!" said Lauren sternly. She proceeded to repeat exactly what he had said to her, in just as angry a voice, all the while wagging her finger reprovingly at him. "Poppa" sat obediently and listened. "Now," said Lauren when she had finished the tirade. "How does that make you feel?"

Rand's shoulders were hunched where he sat. He took a breath and answered sheepishly, "Uh, not very good."

"Well, when you shout at us," continued Lauren, "that's how we feel."

"Hmmm," said her grandfather. "You're right. I'm sorry."

It was a marvelous moment. I was proud of my father-in-law for taking his lumps, and extremely proud of my eight-year-old daughter for standing up to his intimidation. Interestingly, my mother-in-law and sister-in-law were at first horrified. They were shocked by what they felt was Lauren's insubordination. It was unthinkable that a child be allowed to speak so "disrespectfully" to her grandfather, no matter how the grandfather had treated her to start with.

We three women talked quietly about it afterwards, and I think the event caused the others to rethink their default attitudes. Lauren had made them see that children were entitled to be treated as people, and deserved the same consideration as adults. And Rand changed. From that day on, there were no more authoritarian attempts to subdue the grandchildren. If Poppa wanted silence in the cabin so that he could take a nap, he knew he had to speak about his needs respectfully and negotiate with his grandchildren, rather than command them to comply. Lauren continued to be really close to her grandfather until his death six years later. I think he valued her spirit and appreciated the lesson she taught him that day.

The impulse to "discipline" other human beings is most decidedly an impulse to rob them of power. It is top-down relating. All we have to do is imagine how it would feel if the shoe were on the other foot, as Lauren helped her grandfather to do. It never feels good to be bossed or reprimanded, whether we are five years old or fifty.

Radically respectful relationships take time and lots of good will and kindliness. We can't always get our needs met the moment we express them, as my father-in-law learned that rainy afternoon. At least, not without doing harm. We often have to compromise, which means both sides must be willing to listen and learn. When adults are too tired or stressed or in too much of a hurry to express themselves respectfully to their children or grandchildren, they lose out. When they pull rank and force compliance through intimidation, whatever bond once existed begins to wither. I could tell that my neighbour with the troublesome daughter was desperately missing the loving connection mother and child had once shared. Her tough love approach was not repairing the connection with her daughter; it was driving the wedge deeper between them. I wondered whether their relationship would ever recover.

Radical respect requires that we meet one another as true equals. Only when we see each other as equally worthy, equally deserving of consideration, can any meaningful bond grow between us. *Anything less than radical respect undermines intimacy.* A hierarchical, top-down world is not a place where love can thrive. Intimidating, manipulating, criticizing or shaming another person, whether our child, partner, neighbour or work colleague, will eventually kill any chance of meaningful connection between us. People who are treated disrespectfully withdraw from relationships. They feel resentful and scared, rather than safe and supported. No one can love a bully.

Chapter Five
Finding the Jewel

I will not die an unlived life. I will not live in fear of falling or catching fire. I choose to inhabit my days, to allow my living to open me, to make me less afraid, more accessible; to loosen my heart until it becomes a wing.[18]

Dawna Markova

Five years after Lauren quit school, our family decided to quit urban life altogether. We moved to Mayne Island, in the southern Gulf Islands of British Columbia.

Every choice in life, as they say, "makes all the difference." Each decision sets us on a path that veers off into new terrain, revealing further forks in the road that would never have been reached by a different route. Our life stories, you might say, are written with our feet, etched out by our wanderings through the myriad possibilities of experience.

It's tempting to attach a kind of inevitability to our choices. At times it feels as if our stories were somehow written ahead of time, in the stars or in our bones. I suspect this is pure fantasy. Nothing is predestined. However, each instant flows from the one preceding. We arrive here in this present moment by the long circuitous route of all the past moments of our lives. Looking back, we can see that some episodes were crucial in shaping the narrative that followed.

The move to Mayne felt, for me, like fate. I have only felt as powerfully "called" to a decision a few times in my life. The sensation of being impelled towards a life change is peculiar; it is like a pressure in the heart, an upwelling of longing and urgency that can no longer be ignored. Whatever has been brewing, perhaps for years, below the level of conscious thought begins to surface. Awareness shifts. A new sense of meaning emerges, life changes irrevocably.

Here is how it happened. For a couple of years I had been feeling hemmed in by the city. I was spending all my time in the car, driving the girls to various events or to visit friends across town. Although the homeschooling community was lively and stimulating, I felt frustrated with the frenetic lifestyle. There was something missing from our lives. I longed for a greater sense of leisure and spaciousness. I craved a deeper connection to nature and to the rhythms of the day and the seasons.

That year Richard had been quite miserable. He had a long commute through increasingly congested traffic to get to work. And he was finding the work itself stressful and exhausting. Several years earlier he had joined his father's architectural firm, and the strain of working with his sometimes overbearing father, as well as the effort of managing a couple of very demanding clients, had begun to take an emotional and physical toll on him. He suffered from chest pains and insomnia. He talked about the future as if he thought he wouldn't live long. He was only thirty-eight!

One afternoon, while walking back to his car from a Vancouver job site where he was doing an inspection, Richard collapsed on the side of the road. His heart was pounding and he felt short of breath. The world spun around him. He thought he was having a heart attack or a stroke. At the hospital, however, after extensive tests, they could find nothing wrong with him. The doctor told him he'd had a panic attack, but that he was otherwise healthy. His advice was "reduce your stress level." Richard was sent home.

Needless to say, the experience terrified both of us. Something needed to change.

I suggested we both needed a mid-winter break from the city, so we decided to spend a week on Mayne Island.

Richard's grandfather had bought the quarter-section of waterfront and wilderness on Mayne Island back in the 1950s. Over time Richard's parents had cleared twelve acres of pasture. They had also partnered with a neighbour to raise a small flock of sheep on the fields. The extended Iredale family used the Mayne Island property only for holidays. No one had ever lived there. Richard fondly remembers many summers camping on the property as a very young child and, later, staying in a hand-built, non-electrified log cabin set back along the edge of the forest. When our children were young, we would stay for a couple of weeks in that cabin every summer. I loved being on the island. The five of us would spend hours at the beach, clambering over the rocks or digging in the sand. We'd pile in the canoe and paddle along the sandstone cliffs of the bay, or pack a picnic and go exploring in the forest. At night we'd sit around a campfire, cuddled in blankets, and tell stories.

When we arrived that January morning, the log cabin was freezing. We lit the wood stove, boiled the kettle for tea, and ate our lunch while wrapped up in blankets by the fire. Gradually the chill left the air. Outside the cabin windows, the fields and forests were luminously green. The silence was almost tangible. By evening, Richard had begun to relax. His face softened and the deep lines of tension around his eyes disappeared. The girls and I felt it too. The edgy restlessness of city life seemed gradually to ebb from our muscles and bones.

We spent a week reading, walking in the woods or along the beach, playing board games and drawing. Night fell early. By four o'clock we had the coal oil lanterns lit and dinner simmering on the wood stove. By eight o'clock the girls were asleep upstairs under down quilts and Richard and I had a quiet hour or so to ourselves by the fire before we too crept up to bed. The long winter night without lights or TV or radio gave us all permission to get the rest we had been needing for months.

After a couple of days, I began to dread going home. The simplicity of this life was intoxicating. Something deep in my core responded to it, like a root long thirsting for water that finds an underground spring. Towards the end of the week, one question kept arising: Why couldn't we come and live on the island? The girls loved it here. We loved it. The land was free; we could sell our stake in town and have enough money to build our own house. What was stopping us?

Richard and I had actually considered this possibility many times over the years, usually at the end of every visit to the island. But in the past, whenever we started to visualize a new life for our family on Mayne, anxiety would set in. We worried that the girls would miss their city friends and that island life wouldn't offer enough stimulation for them, especially as they grew older. Richard wasn't sure that he would find enough work on the island, and felt scared about losing the excitement and opportunity of a city architectural practice. It was so slow and sleepy on Mayne. We feared we'd all slip into a kind of torpor.

This time it felt different. Richard and I both sensed that he was at risk in the life we were currently living. The strain was becoming unbearable. Something needed to shift for him. I, too, felt stuck. Mayne Island seemed to offer a chance to break some old patterns, to heal and grow. Why couldn't we move to the island for just a year? Even half a year? We could always return to Vancouver if the experiment failed.

Such thoughts were agitating and unsettling. My mind felt like one of those snowglobes I played with as a kid — all the white flakes inside the glass dome shaken up and scattering. My longing was almost palpable. And yet, I wondered, why did I want to make such a big change? Was I crazy? It was so risky and uncertain. In fact, moving to Mayne could be a giant failure that would make us all miserable. Why uproot everyone and start all over?

I think the decision would have been an impossible one to make if it weren't for a pair of horses. By that time, Lauren and Marlise had been in love with horses for a couple of years. Back in the city, I'd been driving them almost an hour each way every week to take horse-riding lessons. They read every book about horses they could find. They drew horses and wrote stories about horses. Lauren told me that the one thing in all the world that would make her the "happiest ever" would be to have her own horse some day.

Here is a journal entry written after a day that changed our lives.

Wednesday, January 20, 1998

What a day, yesterday! Everything is topsy-turvy. I still can't believe it. . . .

On Monday morning Lauren picked up a copy of Island Tides (the inter-island newspaper) that someone had left in the cabin and found an ad for two horses for sale on Galiano. She was so excited! "Listen to this, Mom. They are selling an Arabian mare and a Standardbred gelding. I love Arabians! Can we go see them? What if we bought them and brought them here? We could come and live here too, and ride horses every day. Could we? That's my dream you know. That would be my dream come true!" Marlise chimed in immediately, "Me too! Me too! Oh, can we get horses, Mom?"

Impulsively, I said, "Well, let's go and visit them tomorrow. Why not?" We'd spent a few quiet days at the cabin and I was thinking a day trip to Galiano would be fun for us all. Richard agreed. So early yesterday morning we hopped in the car and caught the ferry. Found the little farm at the end of a long wooded driveway. It was a beautiful place, just a few acres of pasture, some old fruit trees. And in a fenced paddock, two beautiful horses! As we drove up and parked next to the fence, my heart turned over at the sight of them. Needless to say, the girls squealed with delight from the back seat.

The horses were very curious about us and leaned their heads out over the fence as we approached. Doris, their owner, who had been cleaning their little shed, spotted us and came up to make introductions. "Halo" is a sixteen-year-old bay pony, not too small at just over fourteen hands high. "Rasta" is only eight. He is a magnificent, dark-brown fellow, standing over sixteen hands high. After the girls had had a chance to groom and curry the horses, Doris saddled them up and let the girls ride them up and down the driveway and around the small paddock. Rasta seemed a bit high-strung, but Halo was, as Doris said, "bomb-proof." And since Halo was the dominant one in the pair, Rasta went wherever she did.

I still can't get my head around it. We bought them, then and there. It was so impulsive. We arranged with Doris that she keep the horses until April or May, so that we would have a few months to figure things out.

Late last night, when we were all in bed, Richard and I lay awake feeling stunned. What have we done?! It feels like a corner has been turned. There is no going back. But we don't even have a place to live over here. We can't use the cabin full-time, since everyone else in the family wants it too. We'll have to find a place to rent. And how long will we stay? Six months? More? What will we do with the horses when we go back to the city?

Richard especially feels really worried. Moving to Mayne seems suddenly really risky to him. How will we make a life here? Won't the girls get lonely? Where will we live? Questions, questions, and as yet, no clear answers.

The change seemed so huge and sudden that we decided to commit to spending only six months living on Mayne, starting in April. It would give us a taste of country life. Richard would commute to work in Vancouver for part of the week, staying at his parents' house in town, while the girls and I lived full-time on the island. It would be an adventure. We'd return to city life renewed.

Three months later, at the end of April, we packed our bags and left the city, moving into a rented house not far from the family farm. I recall that spring and summer as a period of endlessly sunny days. In fact, there was so little rain for six months that islanders were very worried about the risk of forest fires. Our rented house was right on the water, facing a stony, offshore reef where seals sunbathed and herons rested. Halo and Rasta arrived the first week in May. Every day we walked the half-mile of tree-lined country road over to the farm to feed, groom and ride the horses. It didn't take them long to get used to their new pasture. They quickly learned to ignore the sheep, and to tolerate the fawning attentions of Obadiah, the resident donkey. I had no idea what to do with the horses once the winter came — whether to find someone on the island to look after them while we were in town or take them back to the city and board them. I as yet had no picture of what the future would hold. During those first months I focused on living one day at a time.

The girls loved everything about the horses — from grooming them and picking their hooves to exploring the island roads and trails on horseback. Having their very own horses was a lot different from riding once a week at the riding school in town. Since I myself knew nothing about horses, I found a neighbour down the road who was an avid horsewoman and arranged for her to give Lauren and Marlise regular lessons. But mostly the girls had to learn about grooming, saddling and riding from consulting books and from trial and error. That first summer there were quite a few mishaps! I shudder when I think of some of the falls the girls took. But they seemed undaunted by the scrapes and bruises. They were in love with those horses.

Those first few months on the island passed slowly. Weekends were filled with visits from city friends eager to find out what we were up to. The weather was so warm that we swam almost every day, even in June. It was as if the island was showing us its brightest, loveliest face, and we were all smitten. We never did move back to Vancouver. After two months of this idyllic lifestyle, we all sensed that there was no going back to the old life. We sold our house in town and began building our own home on the family property.

That summer we also became sheep farmers. Ken, our nearest neighbour, had been partnering with my father-in-law to raise sheep on the twelve acres of pasture. Ken was a former ad man for the *Vancouver Sun* newspaper. He and his wife, Karen, had moved to the island in search of a simpler life, and now ran a B&B out of their home. Besides looking after the sheep, Ken raised cockateels and other exotic birds. (Lauren's first summer job a couple of years later was hand-feeding the baby cockateels.) After we'd been living on the island for a month or so, Ken approached me and asked if we would like to take over looking after the sheep. He was feeling overextended. Also, he could tell from how keen the girls were that they would enjoy being shepherdesses. He promised to help us with the first lambing season, and to advise us on sheep care.

That first fall we put the ram into the field with the rest of the flock, and over the next five months watched the ewes grow round and heavy. Lambing season began in February. What an intense and vivid experience! Mostly, the births went easily, but over the subsequent years we had our share of crises. We learned, through hard experience, for instance, that lambs are very vulnerable in the first twenty-four hours of life. If they don't begin to suckle right away, they get hypothermia and die quickly. Each night when we fed the ewes in the barn we counted noses. If a ewe was missing, we took a flashlight out into the field and looked for her. Usually we found her with a newborn or two at her side. Our job then — usually one of the girls helped me — was to gently carry the newborn lambs back to the barn, coaxing the mother to follow. Once back at the barn, we could shut the new family in for the night. Confined together, away from the cold wind, mother and lambs had a greater chance of bonding and surviving that first crucial period.

Sometimes lambs were rejected by their mothers. Sometimes the mothers died before the lambs were weaned. Our first year, we adopted a pair of twin lambs, orphaned at a month old. The girls called the little black ewe-lamb "Flicka" and the ram-lamb "Coolio." We took Flicka and Coolio back to our rented house, built a shelter for them on the outside deck, and fed them lamb formula from beer bottles topped with special lamb nipples. The lambs trotted around after the girls like puppies. Occasionally they would find their way into the house and we would hear the clip clop, clip clip of their small hooves clattering on the tile floor. Flicka grew tall, and soon joined our flock of breeding ewes. Coolio, on the other hand, died prematurely (bottle-fed lambs often seem not to thrive). This was a bit of a relief for me. I didn't know how I was going to tell the girls that we couldn't keep him. They would have been heartbroken to see him loaded into the truck with the other lambs destined for slaughter.

Despite our best efforts, we seemed to lose at least a couple of lambs every season. Occasionally, a ewe died — either from infection after birthing, or from uterine prolapse. I vividly recall one winter afternoon, standing in my gumboots in the barn, listening to the tiny, high-pitched bleating of newborn lambs and the deep, answering calls of their mothers. At my feet lay a dead lamb, slick and already smelling of rot. An exhausted ewe panted on her side nearby. My hands were covered in blood and amniotic fluid. I had had to thrust my hand up inside the ewe to deliver the dead lamb, which had died inside her and was turning septic. There was milk on my hands too, from an earlier session helping another newborn learn to suck. I felt exhausted, sad that I hadn't been able to save the dead lamb, and worried about the ewe. She seemed weak and feverish. But I have never felt more alive than at that moment. Standing there at the crossroads between life and death, I felt awed by the mystery of existence. The beauty and fragility of life filled me with wonder and gratitude.

Looking back, I can't say for absolute certain that moving to Mayne was the right decision. Island life came at a price. After the halcyon days of that first summer, winter arrived. The dark closed in. Our Vancouver friends stopped visiting, and cold and rain often kept us indoors rather than out in the fields and woods, riding and hiking. There were no other homelearning families on the island, and few children the same ages as ours for them to play with. At times the girls were lonely. At times they felt frustrated at the lack of opportunity to take classes in things that interested them, like dance or music or theatre. At times, indeed, I worried we had made a big mistake.

But I have learned that each choice in life comes as a package — the good and the bad, the upside and the downside, are part and parcel of the whole. Our life on Mayne brought tremendous gifts. It also required sacrifices. Some days our needs were met, and some days they were not. At times the lifestyle worked better for one member of the family than another. Still, looking back, I feel no regret. I can't imagine it having been any other way.

The greatest gift for all of us, I think, was the daily attunement with the natural world. Here is a journal entry I wrote that first year.

March 1998

What sustains me is a new, tender, almost awed feeling of rightness here, in these trees and fields, looking out over the rocky stretches of coastline. Our days are punctuated by visitations: deer browsing the roadsides at dawn, eagles soaring on thermal updrafts at high noon, owls calling across the midnight fields. We live with animals. Our dog, three cats, two horses and twenty sheep depend on us for survival. All the wild animals living nearby — the Canada geese that arrive every spring, the otters, mink, raccoons, frogs, crows, herons and the thousands of species of birds that visit our fields — remind us of the cycles of life and death, and of the vast and mysterious world beyond our human concerns. I love being with my kids in this setting. I love how relaxed and open they are here, how free they feel. We get so much physical exercise these days. We are aware of the movement of the sun and the passage of the seasons. All this is worth the price we seem to have to pay: to be a little bit lonely at times.

The close connection to nature slowly changed Richard. At first I was disappointed that he chose in the end not to move his architectural practice to the island. The small community, with its population of only one thousand residents, already had one architect. Richard didn't feel there was enough work to support two, so he decided instead to commute to Vancouver for part of every week, staying two nights at his parents' house. In the beginning, I worried that the weekly commute would only add to his stress level. But, as it turns out, he found the trip from Mayne to Vancouver *less* stressful than the daily commute back and forth through Vancouver traffic had been when we were living on Vancouver's North Shore. Being able to spend four full days on the island every week meant that he had a regular dose of quiet, uninterrupted time both to work more intensively on his design projects, and to hang out with his family far from the noise and pressure of urban life. The coastal landscape has also influenced his architectural vision. He is becoming an expert on "green" building practices and is now an active member of the Canadian Green Building Council. His designs tend to be both energy-conserving and organic in form, patterned on the shapes found in the natural world.

In some ways, the very limitation of life on Mayne was a gift. Our quiet lifestyle left lots of room for exploration and invention. The small community was inclusive and welcoming rather than competitive; anyone could get involved in the little theatre, or join the dance club, or play music at the Folk Club open mic. One St. Patrick's Day, all three girls performed in an Irish Dance show, dressed in green velvet dresses and purple silk sashes. The show was part of an elaborate Irish Ceili organized by an island schoolteacher, who taught Irish dance classes to the community every Tuesday evening. Lauren, Marlise and I also found opportunities, which we'd never have had in the city, to play and perform music. The older two girls sang and played guitar for several years in a row at an annual island-wide party that featured an entire evening of local music. In our second year on the island, Marlise and I joined a recorder ensemble.

A year later, we formed a five-person Celtic-bluegrass band called Roaring Jelly, which included Marlise's friend Zoe, her mother Yvette and my nephew Adam. Roaring Jelly even recorded a CD in a local recording studio.

Marlise recalls a formative musical experience one day when she was about fourteen years old. The well-known children's troubadour Raffi had moved to the island. Marlise, Zoe and their friend Michelle were travelling in a small motor-boat with Raffi and Zoe's dad, Terry, on their way back from a birthday party on Pender Island. The boat broke down partway home. At first the little band of seafarers was very dismayed. A gentle rain had started to fall. They had no cell phone, and therefore no way to get help. Terry got to work tinkering with the motor, while the others, sitting in the front of the boat, pulled an oilskin over their knees and began to sing. Bobbing on the wide, empty sea, beneath a drizzling, cold grey sky, Raffi and the three girls "vocal jammed" — as Marlise described it — for over two hours. Finally Terry got the motor running again, just in time before dark. Marlise came home beaming. She said she had forgotten all about the cold and the danger because singing with Raffi out on the sea had been so magical. Being able to jam with an expert musician that day showed her what possibilities music could afford. She felt inspired to immediately write a song about the experience.

Small-town life suited me more than did the pressure and anonymity of the city. I loved shopping for groceries in the local store and greeting the store clerk by name. I felt grateful to live in a community where you smile at everyone you pass on the road or pathways, whether you know them or not, where neighbours bring food or raise money for someone who is ill or going through hard times, and where, despite the inevitable conflicts and disagreements that come from living together, there is a great deal of forgiveness and loyalty.

Mayne Island turned out to be a safe place for us all to dive deeper into our own playfulness. When Roaring Jelly disbanded (because the three teenagers started their own band, Bell Jar) I formed a Celtic-jazz trio, Jaiya, along with two island musicians.

I began composing, performing and recording my own music; I also took up acting and mime and dance — and returned to my first love, writing.

I can't say for certain that I needed to leave the city in order to unleash my pent-up creativity. Perhaps I just needed a radical change. I needed to leave behind that old story of the shy and overly sensitive Lael and re-invent myself. Mayne Island just happened along at the right moment. It has been for me like the hermetic vase of the alchemist: a place of transformation, where I found the "gold" of aliveness. Now that the girls are grown, I feel drawn to exploring adventures off the island, and spend part of each week involved in city-based activities, but Mayne Island will always be home. It is my heart-place; when I gaze out over our fields at the sea, I am reminded of what truly matters to me.

Another gift of our move to Mayne has been a closer connection with Richard's extended family. Richard's brother, Tab, and his sister, Jennifer, as well as Richard's parents while they were alive, share the Mayne property with us. Jennifer and her husband, Peter, built a cottage on the island the same year that we built our house. Tab and his wife, Paddy, after spending their holidays in the log cabin, are now also building their own place here, and look forward to living on the island part-time once they retire. Between them, the three siblings have eight children, all close in age, who have grown up spending summers on the island. Tab has three sons, Ben, Rylan and Brodey, while Jennifer has a son, Adam, and a daughter, Meg. The eight cousins all seem very attached to Mayne. The property has become the gathering place for the clan.

Until the cousins were in their late teens and getting busy with other activities, we often had birthdays, Thanksgiving and Christmas together on the island. We designed our house to have a large dining room, with a table (built by my father) that could extend to sit eighteen people. That table has seen many lively family dinners over the years — gatherings which gave the generations a chance to mingle with one another. In summers the extended family together hosted an annual "lamb bake," a huge event which took place outside the log cabin, and to which we invited relatives and friends, both from on and off the island. We roasted one of our largest lambs on a spit over coals (my brother-in-law Tab would get up at 6 a.m. to start turning the crank). We set up long tables outside and had a potluck feast. After dinner there was always a campfire and a sing-along that evolved over the years into a sophisticated music jam as the cousins got older and began to play instruments.

Mayne Island turned out to be pivotal in the lives of Adam and Meg in particular. My nephew and niece had been unhappy at school and had been asking for a year or two to be allowed to learn at home like their cousins. Jennifer and Peter worked full-time in Victoria, so they had never thought it possible to allow the kids to drop out. But once we lived nearby on the island, Jennifer was able to do some juggling to make the lifestyle work. She managed to persuade her boss to allow her to work from her cottage on Mayne two days a week. The other two days her kids stayed at our house on the island while she commuted back to Victoria. On Fridays they all went back home to the city to spend the weekend with Peter.

My daughters loved this arrangement. The cousins were their good friends, and the five children formed a lively community for each other for a few years. During those years there was no typical day in our life on Mayne. A lot depended on the weather. On fair-weather days, the cousins saddled and took turns riding the horses, or played outside in the fields and woods. In the course of a couple of years they had explored every inch of our eighty-acre property and had given special names to every rock and glade. The younger two, Julia and Meg, even had their own secret world — "the Forestorium" — that they would visit on their own whenever the older kids were busy doing something else. Sometimes they walked a couple of kilometres to the Trading Post to buy chocolate bars or ice cream, either all five together or in pairs. On rainy days they drew and painted, read, discussed books, played board games and, of course, squabbled with each other like siblings! They shared a common passion for the horses and all helped to tend the sheep.

Adam and Meg thrived on their new freedom. Both have grown up to become conscientious, talented and highly inner-directed young adults. Adam, now twenty-five, is a sought-after professional musician, recording engineer and impresario who organizes a thriving annual music festival on Mayne Island. Meg is a fine singer-songwriter who has toured Canada several times. She is also an apprentice carpenter as well as, at the age of twenty-three, part owner and manager of a restaurant/music-venue in Victoria.

Island life was a work in progress, one that needed constant adjusting as our needs changed. Once they were older, Adam and Meg got busy with music lessons and part-time jobs in Victoria and came less often to the island. My daughters, as well, began to spend quite a bit of time on ferries travelling first back to Vancouver and then to Victoria so they could participate in activities with other homelearning kids, or take classes in music or theatre or dance. Since there were no other unschooling families on Mayne I began a weekly creative writing group for about ten homeschoolers in Victoria, which both Julia and Marlise also attended. Later, as the teenagers got older, this evolved into a philosophy discussion group in which we read and debated topics ranging from Socrates' concept of self-knowledge to feminist political theory to Buddhism.

Both Lauren and Marlise at one stage elected to take the water taxi to high school on Salt Spring Island — Lauren for grades eleven and twelve, and Marlise for grade ten. They were curious about meeting other teenagers and wanted to see for themselves what high school was all about. Lauren stuck it out for two years. Marlise, although she made many friends and particularly enjoyed being in the jazz choir, found the social and intellectual atmosphere of school stultifying; she quit after a year. Julia never chose to go to public school at all. Like her sisters, however, she was ready and eager to leave Mayne for the big city. She moved to Vancouver to go to college when she was eighteen.

Though they've moved on, all three girls are still very attached to the island. They seem to come back whenever they feel stressed or ungrounded, knowing that spending a few days surrounded by sea and woods and wildlife will help restore their sense of well-being. They are at home in this geography. They are comfortable bushwhacking through forest undergrowth or scrambling over sandstone rocks on the beach. The rhythms of life here have shaped them: the long summer days spent on the beach or building forts in the woods, the summer nights skinny-dipping in the phosphorescent ocean or sleeping out under the stars, as well as the quiet winter evenings making endless pots of tea and reading by the fire. They have tasted a slower pace of life, and know that it will be here waiting for them whenever they might wish to return to it.

Finding the Inner Voice

By Richard Iredale

Insert 1

I vividly remember one morning in February 1993 when I found Lauren, then a skinny seven-year-old, hiding in the basement of our house in Vancouver. She didn't want to go to school. I had looked for her all over the house. Finally, I found her in the shadows cowering behind an upright piece of plywood, her thin little body shaking with fear. I regret now to admit that I pulled her out of her hiding place and angrily insisted that she go to school.

All of grade two was a battle for us, and kindergarten and grade one hadn't been much better. Lauren didn't take to French-immersion kindergarten, which, being typical parents of our generation, we had thought would be great. When we transferred her into "regular" kindergarten in January, most of the friends had already paired off and she spent her first school year as an outsider. Things didn't get much better in grade one. When in grade two she finally did connect with a couple of girls at school, the friendship was short-lived. The other girls tolerated Lauren as "third girl" of their little group for four months and then, one day in early February, decided (for whatever playground reasons) that she had to go. They announced this to her at recess the next day. She was no longer their friend. She couldn't play with them any more, they said. In fact, they wanted her to stay on the other side of the playground during recess and lunch.

It wasn't until Lauren was twenty-five that she actually told me this story. She suddenly remembered everything. She spoke with a tight voice as she wondered how her child-self had coped with the rejection and aloneness.

At seven, Lauren did not know how to explain her predicament, either to herself or to us. It wasn't until the teachers went on strike for two months in May of 1993 that we began to question sending Lauren to school. That was the turning point that led to everything in this book. That's when the penny finally dropped. Lauren had been trying to tell us all along that school wasn't working for her, and all along we had been ignoring her discomfort. Now we had a chance to set things right. Most importantly, I saw that Lauren had an opportunity to learn from this crisis an invaluable life lesson: If something is not working, change it. Be creative. Keep trying new solutions until you find one that fits.

In order to know if something is not working for you, you have to be able to trust your feelings. I believe that each of us is born with an *inner voice* that points us in the right direction, but we learn to ignore it in the course of our childhood and adolescence. I've found this in my own life. I've worked for years as a landscape painter and architect. I have taken countless wrong turns when it comes to design. I have made mistakes and had a few disasters. Gradually I've learned to listen for those ever-so-quiet whispers. The inner voice seems to come from deep inside my body, in the realm of feelings and the unconscious. When I stop and really listen to this inner guidance, things turn out much better than if I ignore its wisdom. Yoda, in the movie *Star Wars*, had it right when he urged the hero, Luke Skywalker, to "feel the Force." Luke had to learn to let go of what he *thought* he should do, and instead follow his heart. The Force has to be *felt*.

It's a very quiet, very deep kind of intuition. It guides us towards a rich and fulfilling life.

My nervous collapse at the age of thirty-eight, which led to our family's move to Mayne Island, was a wake-up call for me. Driving back from a stressful meeting one day, in heavy traffic, I had what felt like a heart attack and ended up pulling over and lying down on a grassy boulevard. I spent about an hour staring at a few blades of grass, waiting to die, before I dragged myself into a schoolyard and asked the attendant to call an ambulance. For three years after that terrible day I suffered from intense chest pains that I feared would kill me. I really didn't know what to do. It wasn't until Lael, always the courageous one in our family, suggested that we move out to the quiet serenity of Mayne Island that I found a way forward. For the first two years I spent part of each week there building a house, which gave me lots of physical work to do. Many weekends I would work alone clearing up around the site, digging holes or installing insulation. One day, about a year after we moved, I stood in the forest and looked across the field at the nearly finished house. The rain was falling and clouds were moving overhead among the cedar trees. All of a sudden the pain lifted from my chest — and I knew it was gone forever.

For twenty years I had pushed myself too hard. I had been a good student at school, and a good son living up to my parents' expectations. I hadn't always known how to make choices that were good for me. I hadn't always felt the Force. Gradually, I've been learning to live a more balanced life, with physical activity (mostly hiking and gardening), mind work and rest in equal measure. Now, whether I am designing a new building or trying to resolve a conflict with a client or just walking in the forest, I listen for guidance from that very quiet voice inside. It whispers truth and inspiration to me: Do this, not that. Say this, not that. Go here, not there.

I believe that *knowing how you feel* is crucial to living well. Feelings are our guides. They tell us when someone is safe or dangerous, when someone is truthful or dishonest, when our boundaries are being quietly invaded, and what is the *right* thing to do. For an architect or artist, they tell us what is beautiful or not. The emotional content of childhood and youth is so important because we learn early whether to listen to our feelings or to ignore them. Sadly, most of us lose touch with our feelings because we are constantly asked to do things that go against the grain.

Ultimately you can either learn to listen to your feelings or learn to ignore them. Since society forces so many people to put up with loneliness, isolation and humiliation and to soldier on anyway, it's no wonder there is so much anger and hatred in the world. I cringe to think of all the millions of children who were taught that they are outsiders, of no account, and that their thoughts and feelings don't matter.

When we took Lauren out of school, we decided to let her act on what her inner voice was telling her. She knew that school wasn't a good place for her to be at that point in her life. Her heart didn't feel safe or inspired or welcome there. She had to leave in order to go forward. She has been following her inner voice ever since. With its guidance, she has been designing a life that for her feels good and true and right.

Chapter Six
Curriculum: See How They Run!

The trouble with the rat race is that even if you win, you're still a rat.[19]

Lily Tomlin

My choice not to school my children was a choice to give up following a fixed curriculum. My daughters never learned at the age of eleven, for instance, what the exports of Japan are. They can't name all the past prime ministers of Canada (nor can I). I am sure there are whole sections of the miraculous, almost infinitely varied terrain of human knowledge that they have "missed" in the years of their growing up. But there are other whole landscapes that they have thoroughly explored. Each new interest or curiosity has led to further interests and explorations in a marvelously meandering, unpredictable and highly personal way. Over years of observing, questioning and experimenting, they have built for themselves a coherent picture of the world — one that they constantly revise and deepen with each new experience.

When Lauren didn't go back to school for grade four, a friend expressed concern. "Once kids get to grade four it's no longer just fun and games," she worried. "They begin to cover a lot of *content*." I was quite baffled by her statement. Did she think that Lauren's unstructured days were somehow content-free? Obviously she believed that only a few specific things are essential to know about. All the rest is "extracurricular."

The word "curriculum" derives from the Latin *currerre*, meaning "to run." Originally it meant "the route or course a runner takes in a race." When educators design the curriculum for each school grade or stage of development they are mapping out a specific trail that all students "should" follow through the landscape of knowledge. They believe that to become an educated person one must travel this particular road.

For me, there are three flaws in this notion: First, it makes learning a race. It sets up a paradigm of competition, of rushing towards the finish line in order to win the prize. If there is only one path for learning and growth, children will naturally compare how far along it they are with respect to their peers. They will begin to feel either like losers or winners in the race for skills and knowledge.

Second, I find the notion that there is one right path to knowledge downright absurd. The world is vast and complex. There must be an almost infinite amount of information that could be known about the universe. Why should we privilege a small subset of knowledge as necessary or real or valuable — make it the sanctioned "content" that all educated people must learn — and call the rest optional? Who decided, for instance, that all children should learn algebra, but not organic gardening or carpentry or healthy cooking? Why are art and music and dance considered less important than science?

Third, children simply do not retain learning when they aren't engaged. Children readily absorb and remember information about their favourite things. When they *need to know more* about some aspect of their world right now, they are relentless investigators. But ply them with bits and bites of information about subjects they have not yet — and perhaps never will — become fascinated by and you are wasting your breath. They may oblige you by temporarily memorizing uninteresting facts for a test, but after a couple of weeks they won't recall any of it.

School curricula change over time, and reflect the cultural fashions of the day. A hundred years ago, Latin and Rhetoric formed the backbone of classroom content. In another hundred years, schools may require that all children learn yoga or meditation. What alarms me is that, in each new generation, we unquestioningly allow a few people to decide for the rest of us what matters most.

When I was still trying to "teach" my kids I kept coming up against this fundamental uncertainty: I had no real idea who my children would grow up to be or what kind of world they would inherit. If they were going to be engineers, yes, they would eventually need some skill at math. If they were going to be organic farmers, they would one day need to learn about soil and integrated pest management. If they aspired to be writers, they would probably need to master the rules of spelling and grammar. But at the time, my children were only three, six and eight! Who could possibly tell how their spirits would evolve? I had no guarantee that I knew better than they what knowledge would turn out to be useful.

I realized this simple truth: *I had no way of knowing where my daughters would be in twenty years. I only knew where they were right then and there, in that exact moment.* If I relaxed and listened, my kids would show me what they wanted to learn. They had their own questions to ask. When I allowed them to follow their curiosity, they learned quickly and efficiently and retained what they learned.

John Holt said, "When a child is doing something she's passionately interested in, she grows like a tree — in all directions. This is how children learn, how children grow. They send down a taproot like a tree in dry soil. The tree may be stunted, but it sends out these roots, and suddenly one of these little taproots goes down and strikes a source of water. And the whole tree grows."[20] We can't tell ahead of time which underground spring will nourish our children's spirit and cause them to flourish. We can't prescribe the best way for them to grow. They have to feel their own way.

Sometimes the paths my daughters' learning took seemed very random. One week one would pore over library books about dolphins, and the next week another would want to read about Greek myths. Now and again I would observe that one or the other child had become hooked. Something had caught hold of her, addressed her heart, and she would binge for weeks or months or sometimes years on that one interest or activity.

When Lauren was eight, she discovered the graphic fantasy world of *Elfquest*, created by Wendy Pini. For the next four years, she had two main subjects in her personal curriculum: horses and *Elfquest*. The world of *Elfquest* had a profound impact on her imagination. She learned to draw by imitating Wendy Pini's figures. Even as an adult, the designs she creates for her silk-screening business still bear the imprint of Wendy Pini's early influence. When Lauren got married last summer, her wedding dress was like something one of the Wolfrider elves would have been proud to wear! Lauren learned to write by crafting her own stories peopled with characters from the *Elfquest* world. She endlessly pondered the value system, lifestyle and social organization of the Wolfriders and compared it with our own. She even inspired other groups of children at various homelearning events to recreate the world in their collective play.

At times well-meaning relatives would visit and comment that Lauren didn't seem to be reading anything other than fantasy. "Shouldn't she be broadening her horizons?" they'd ask. "What about literature and science?"

By that time I knew to be patient. I had observed that each door opened leads to further doors in the unfolding of human curiosity. Sure enough, by thirteen, Lauren was starting to explore other books. At age twenty-seven she is one of the most voracious and omnivorous readers I know. She and her husband, Blake, seem to spend at least a couple of hours each day reading, and the topics that fascinate them range from fiction to physics to world history to political science and everything in between. The *Elfquest* series didn't limit her horizons at all. Instead she discovered the thrill of exploring alternative worlds represented in story and art, a delight she has carried into adulthood.

At one stage of her childhood, Julia's self-designed curriculum centered on maps. Instead of drawing people and animals like her older sisters often did, Julia created complex diagrams of imaginary worlds. These maps were highly detailed, with many winding roads amid forests and houses and castles. She liked to show me her maps and describe to me all the details of these imaginary landscapes.

When she was nine Julia fell in love with a large-format children's atlas of the world that all three girls had been given for Christmas. Lauren and Marlise only flipped through the atlas a few times before losing interest. Julia, however, was fascinated. I can still vividly picture her sitting on our living room couch, her waist-long fair hair forming a curtain over her face as she bent over the beautifully coloured maps and diagrams. She memorized the shapes of the continents and the names of the oceans. She took note of the animals and plants depicted in the margins and asked questions about them. She even asked me to quiz her on the capital cities of the countries in Europe.

She and I decided to create a map of our farm, noting each important place on the eighty-acre property. The map, which still hangs on our wall, is large and highly detailed. Julia painstakingly printed most of the place names (including names she and her sisters and cousins had invented for special boulders or mossy knolls or groves of trees on the property) in her slightly wobbly nine-year-old hand. The map will be a treasure, I believe, for generations.

Julia's interest in maps waned with time. She fell in love with books, discovered journaling and began painting and drawing. But her passion for geography resurfaced at seventeen, when she saved enough money working in a coffee shop to travel with a friend for four months in England, Scotland, Holland, Belgium and France. In the past few years, Julia has become a serious artist and is now majoring in Illustration at Emily Carr University.

For years her art was filled with geographical imagery. On my wall hangs one of her early paintings, depicting an anatomically-correct human heart superimposed by the image of a compass showing north, south, east and west. Lately she has been exploring landscapes of all kinds. She depicts people and animals in the context of their settings, so that the landscape itself becomes as important an element as the central figure.

In the child's interests lie seeds that often flower later into adult life-callings. As a young child Marlise was the queen of imaginative play. The dress-up box was always open. She would spend hours with her sisters and with her friend Michelle — another life-learning child — dressing up in outrageous costumes and "putting on shows," whether an audience was on hand to watch or not. I have a photograph of Marlise and Michelle hamming it up in our living room. Marlise has a tiara mounted on her wispy, white-blonde hair, and a purple feather boa around her neck. Her hands are on her hips and her eyebrows are raised with the arch, haughty look of a grand-dame. Michelle is wearing a florescent pink leotard and a flouncy skirt, and has a flowery hat perched rakishly on her dark curls. There is such energy in the picture — the girls look as if they are about to burst into song, or begin dancing or leaping. Their young bodies visibly shimmer with excitement and enthusiasm.

Here is an entry from my journal, July 1994. Marlise was six years old.

> *Today was one of those magical summer days. Saturday. Marlise, Lauren, Meghan and some other kids from down the lane were playing outside on the front boulevard. I was upstairs reading Julia a story, listening with half an ear to the laughter and shouts from outside as the girls played up and down the street in the glorious sunshine.*
>
> *Suddenly I heard a desperate weeping. "Mommy, Mo-o-mmyyyy!" It was Marlise, wailing and sobbing as if the world had just come to an end. I leapt to my feet, hurried down the stairs and out the door, heart racing.*

Marlise was sitting slumped against the trunk of a tree, tears streaming down her face, a picture of abject despair.

"Marlise! What happened, sweetheart?" I called out as I ran to comfort her. Suddenly her head snapped up towards me. It was as if she were waking from a trance.

"What do you want?" she said, frowning. I stopped, surprised.

"You were crying! I thought you were hurt."

Marlise got to her feet, all trace of desperation gone. She seemed unbothered by the fat tears still sliding down her cheeks.

"I was playing, Mom. It's in the game. Don't you see?" she explained condescendingly, as if I were a simpleton. "I am the daughter and my mommy has just died. So now I'm an orphan and everything. Now go away."

"Mo-mmy!" she began to wail again, instantly back in character. Lauren and the other children appeared from around the back of the house and hurried towards her, evidently not at all surprised by her display of woe.

I skulked back to the house feeling rather sheepish, hoping none of my neighbours had witnessed our exchange. I had been fooled by an impressive bit of acting on the part of my six-year-old daughter. What an Oscar-worthy performance!

Both Marlise and Michelle have ended up pursuing careers in performance. Michelle completed a theatre degree at UBC and is now an active performer and composer in Vancouver. Marlise (whose stage name is Marley Daemon) is a professional musician and clown. She has acted in plays, taken extensive clowning workshops and become very comfortable on stage; she loves interacting with an audience. She is also interested in studying Expressive Arts Therapy and hopes to use theatre and music to help others connect with what she calls their "body of delight."

"Performing arts" turned out to be one of the main areas of "content" in her childhood curriculum. All those years of spontaneous dramatic play built skills that are proving useful in her adult life.

Sometimes we can introduce our children to new interests, especially when we ourselves are keen. But despite our own delight in an activity, our children may remain unmoved. Richard likes to tell the story of his visit to the hobby store with Lauren when she was nine years old. One of Richard's passions as a child had been model building. He remembers never being happier as a boy than when he had a new model car or plane or boat to build from a kit. He realizes now that all his early practice in 3-D modeling stood him in good stead when, as an adult, he chose to study architecture. At the time, however, model building was just pure delight for him. He had no thought of "preparing" for the future.

Since Richard had been so keen on model building, he naturally assumed that Lauren would be too. For her ninth birthday, he offered to buy her a model of her choosing. They drove downtown to the biggest hobby shop in the area. Richard bounded through the door, eager to show Lauren how many choices there were. First they scanned the rows of cars, both antique and modern. Then they perused the shelves of boats and trains and airplanes. They checked out the submarines and the spacecraft. There were so many varieties, shapes, sizes and colours. Richard was in heaven!

"Which one would you like?" he asked Lauren. "I'll buy it for you and we'll work on it together." He felt the old excitement returning at the thought of bringing one of those shiny boxes home, disgorging its contents onto the dining room table and then spending happy, absorbed hours piecing the hundreds of small parts carefully together. . . .

Lauren hesitated, frowning. Then she looked up at her father and said, "Is that all they've got? Is it all just about *transportation*? Have they got any *animals*, for instance? Horses, maybe?"

Richard was shocked. He'd never thought of his models as all having to do with "transportation." But it was true. Lauren was clearly not particularly keen on things with wheels and gears. None of those vehicles in the shiny boxes stirred her imagination or touched her heart. They just weren't on her personal curriculum, thank you very much!

The store clerk, when asked, managed to find a dust-covered model kit of a horse in the back of the shop. Lauren happily took that home, and Richard helped her build it. But it was the only model she ever made. One was enough, since modeling itself was not what drove her curiosity.

Fulfilling our "potential" as human beings involves allowing what is *alive* in us to flourish. A child's passion and curiosity will call her forth into the world. She doesn't need to be shown the right way. In her own sweet time, she'll chart her own course through the abundant wilderness of Being.

Chapter Seven
Play

Let my playing be my learning, and my learning be my playing.[21]

Johan Huizinga

By 1995, we had been unschooling for a couple of years. I had learned to trust that play is a serious vehicle of growth and learning.

Here is a journal entry from the spring of 1995. The girls were nine, seven and four:

Right now Lauren, Marlise and Julia along with neighbours Meghan, Patrick and Matthew are outside with their Playmobile figures, creating a series of elaborate farms, cattle ranches and horse-rings in the grass around the birch tree on our boulevard. Their minds are pulsing. The energy of their concentration radiates from the sphere of their play, almost like a halo of light around them as I watch out the window. They are working deeply and intensively at this process of constructing an entire world — complete with its own people and history and "problems" to solve (the kids love solving "problems"!) — out of a few odds and ends of toys and grass and sticks and rocks.

Although the children vary in age from four to ten they are collaborating harmoniously. I just heard Julia shout excitedly, "Let's make this the horse hospital!" Now she is busy making little beds of moss for all the "sick" animals. Now Marlise is bringing over two injured animals and there is much concerned chatter between the two girls about what medicine to administer . . .

The etymology of the word "play" is enlightening. The Old English word *plegian* from which our word play is derived originally meant "to move about briskly, to frolic" and was related to the Old German word *plegan* meaning "to rejoice, to be glad." "Play" implies movement, process, energetic activity that is not a means to an end, but a source of delight in itself. To engage in play is to be completely absorbed in the present moment, without anxiety about the future or regret about the past.

The word "work," in contrast, is related to the word "urge." Both in turn are related to the Old English *wrecan* which means "drive, pursue, hunt." Work connotes "urgency" — a "drive" to be somewhere else than the present moment. We tend to think of work as goal-oriented activity that is never done for its own sake. Work promises future benefit rather than present delight.

Parents have often asked me over the years how my children will ever know how to "work" if they have been free to play during their whole childhood. They tell me that adult life is full of boring or painful tasks that can't be avoided, and that children who are allowed to "just do whatever they feel like" will never acquire the discipline to do what *needs* to be done. One woman, a lovely, energetic schoolteacher who taught an after-school Irish dance class that we all participated in for a few years, said emphatically, "I am so lazy, if I was never made to do things, I wouldn't do anything at all."

Where does this bleak view of human nature come from? First of all, I don't believe for a minute that my Irish dancing friend would do "nothing at all" if she felt free to do as she liked. I suspect that she, like everyone, wants to live a meaningful, engaging and fulfilling life. Assuming that people have to be "made" to seek fulfillment makes no sense to me at all. It is like saying a sunflower won't turn towards the sunlight on its own. If my friend realized that she was truly free she might eventually choose to live a *different* life than the one she has been trained for. Once she felt master of her own fate, moreover, she would very likely stop calling her natural impulses "lazy."

That, I think, is the key. If we are free to choose what activities we engage in, we soon stop dividing life into the "good" parts and the "bad" parts. We stop feeling bossed around and resistant. If we want to run in a marathon, for instance, we accept all the effort that goes into training for it. If we want to perform our favourite music on the violin, we accept the need to strengthen our fingers by playing a lot. If we want a bigger house or fancier furniture, we can choose to spend more time earning the money to pay for it all. The "work" or effort or challenge involved in creating a desired way of life can't be separated from the pleasure and satisfaction that lifestyle brings. They are part and parcel of a whole.

When Marlise began taking piano lessons at age six or seven, I decided never to use the "p" word. P for "practice," that is. My feeling was that if Marlise wanted to play the piano, she would play it. If she lost interest in playing, that was fine too. Making "practising" a duty or obligation seemed guaranteed to rob her of her own reasons for playing music.

Marlise is now a very accomplished musician. She seems to be able to pick up just about any instrument she comes across and play it competently. Along with learning piano, she taught herself the penny whistle at age ten and the guitar at thirteen, enrolled in the Victoria Conservatory of Music's Diploma in Jazz program at eighteen, recorded her first CD at twenty-one and at twenty-five is beginning to earn her own living performing and teaching music. She has composed her own songs, always with complex, thoughtful lyrics, for as long as I can remember.

Over the years I have watched many of my friends and neighbours battle with their children over practice time. They would threaten to stop paying for lessons if their child didn't manage at least a certain number of minutes a day. The child, feeling pressured and manipulated, would wail and rage. She would submit for a week or two, then the battle would begin again. Misery all around! I would try to suggest that if all the child did each week was attend the lesson, at least he or she had that half-hour of weekly exposure to music. Wasn't that better than no music at all? "But they are not progressing!" would come the distressed reply. "Why should I keep paying, if they are not going to work hard?"

Marlise's "progress" was patchy and intermittent, since her passion for the piano tended to ebb and flow. There were periods when she didn't seem to want to play much, and others when she was suddenly very keen again. She had a number of different teachers and their attitude would always affect her. One teacher, a former professional musician who, as far as I could tell, didn't *enjoy* music at all, scolded Marlise continually for not practising enough. She said dark and sour things like, "You'll never get good enough to do anything with music if you don't play scales every day." Needless to say, this gloomy attitude led Marlise eventually to quit. Luckily, a year later another teacher moved to the island and Marlise began again. Though I knew Marlise had a lot of talent, I tried to stay very neutral. Whether she ever became a competent musician or not didn't matter. What mattered was that she was growing and exploring and having fun.

"Work" and "play" as opposing concepts belong to a life-denying, oppressive view of the world. When we talk of what we do as "work" we are thinking like slaves. Don't we want to see ourselves as people who are free to shape our lives? How we speak about our choices should reflect our freedom. I am sure that each of us wants to design a life that is meaningful and beautiful, one that we can share with others joyfully. We deserve a language that celebrates our power.

We need a new word that blends the two concepts of work and play: a word that connotes "purposeful activity that is freely chosen and that enriches life." Joseph Campbell sums up the idea in a phrase: "following your bliss." Others have called this experience "flow." When we are fully engaged in the activity of being alive, when we are "caught up" or "taken over" by what we are doing, we don't begrudge the effort involved. The energy involved in the doing and the satisfaction it brings are two sides of the same coin. Whenever Marlise has written a new song, for instance, I will hear her play it over and over again, hammering out the fingering, getting the vocals just right, rewriting the lyrics until she is satisfied. Is she working or playing? If you asked her she would likely give you a blank look. All she knows is that she is *living*, intensely and vividly. She is fully absorbed in the flow of her own creative energy. I suspect it doesn't get much better than that.

Children easily get absorbed by an activity they enjoy. They also love being around absorbed, creatively engaged adults. On an afternoon in August 1995, when our family was spending a couple of weeks holidaying on Mayne Island, I described this scene in my journal:

> *Richard, Lauren and Marlise are all sitting at the table painting with watercolours. Richard gave each of the girls one of his expensive sheets of Arches watercolour paper. Lauren is painting the big arbutus tree by the cabin — she's getting the bark beautifully, with the gold-red-brown streaks. Richard gives her tips if she asks for them. Marlise is working on a very detailed study of the wood stove and the wood box and the wall behind with the mounted lantern and Grannie's Norman Rockwell plates. She has just finished the drawing and is now beginning to paint. Lots of discussion about mixing colours, doing "washes" etc. Richard is busy on his picture based on our recent trip to the Chilcotin: it's a scene of the three girls in a hay field by an old fence, with a fabulous craggy cliff beyond.*
>
> *I love to listen to the three of them chatter happily as they paint side by side. The "teaching" that is going on is really just respectful exchanging of ideas, passing on of experience.*

The girls are fascinated by Richard's picture.
Lauren: "Did you copy that from a photo, Dad?"
Richard (painting all the while he speaks): "Well, no, not
really. I took a lot of photos and they give me ideas, but
the painting really comes out of my imagination. I like to
look at reality and then try to make something even more
beautiful than reality."
Marlise: "How do you make shadow colours?"
Richard: "Try mixing a little orange or gold into some grey."
Marlise: "Gold isn't shadow!"
Richard: "Well, try a little blue then, if you think that would
be better. Do it however you feel like. There's no right way.
Have fun with the colours. See, I'm just experimenting. I
just mess around and see what works."

I love this portrait of three people enjoying each other's companionship and support as they each pursue their own creative project. Richard and the girls here are engaged in a kind of "parallel play" — each, though doing their own thing, is inspired and energized by the presence of the others. Richard, being older and having experimented much more with painting, is able to share some information with his daughters about the ways watercolours interact with paper, and about how colours mix together to form new colours. But he is not there to teach the girls. He is busy with his own work. The girls in turn are drawn to his concentration and his evident enjoyment of painting and want to explore this intriguing activity for themselves. They are "intrinsically motivated," to use Kohn's term — they aren't trying to please anyone by painting a "good" picture. And yet, being in the company of an adult artist is very exciting for them. The atmosphere is light and relaxed, unmarred by anxiety, and yet focused and purposive. An ideal learning environment!

We all, I believe, want our children to take both pride and pleasure in what they do. We hope they develop the capacity to pursue their goals with energy and enthusiasm. Sadly, it is very easy to nip in the bud a child's capacity to engage joyfully with the world. When we over-organize their time, or offer unasked-for "help" or advice, or become too invested in whether they are "good" at any given activity, we prune away their natural exuberance. We make them wary and cautious, instead of bold and resilient. If we want, instead, to empower our children to build meaningful and interesting lives for themselves — to find their true "work" — it is *crucial*, I believe, *to allow them to play*. And we should allow ourselves to play alongside them. We are their best models. When they see us engaging playfully with our own lives — trying new things, "messing around," exploring, learning, improvising, inventing, making mistakes and carrying on — our children realize that they can do the same. They will see from our example that being swept up in the doing of an activity is one of life's great joys. They will feel free to find their own unique way to flow.

Chapter Eight
The Three Rs

Don't let schooling interfere with your education.[22]

Mark Twain

In our early days of learning without schooling I often fretted over the "three Rs." I knew I wanted to allow the girls to learn from life, but I couldn't help worrying that they might never, naturally, learn to read and write well or feel at home with math.

I am glad those years of uncertainty are now fully over. I can breathe a big sigh of relief knowing that my unusual approach to education has "worked," at least as far as readin', ritin' and 'rithmetic go. My three daughters are fully literate. They still, like I do, spell the occasional word wrong, but all three have passed college-level English classes with no problem. They are voracious readers both of fiction and non-fiction. Lauren and Julia both wrote full-length novels during their teen years. Marlise has filled countless volumes with poetry and song lyrics.

How did they learn to read and write? Well, all I can say is that it all just, kind of, *happened*. From the time they were toddlers Richard and I read aloud to them. We all loved to curl up together beside a fire in the evening, sharing an engrossing saga such as the tales of *Pippi Longstocking* or *The Lord of the Rings* or *The Golden Compass*. The girls also had lots of opportunity to see their parents reading. They knew that books contained whole universes just waiting to be explored.

Although Lauren went to school until grade two, the younger girls were never "taught" to read. Reading came naturally, with no struggle or stress. By the age of five or six they began to be curious about letters. They wanted to know what sounds certain letters made, and how to string those sounds together into words. I would "help" them when they asked for it, but mostly I tried to be patient and let them come to reading in their own time. For both Marlise and Julia, the final leap into competent literacy happened suddenly and unexpectedly, between the age of seven and eight.

Here is a journal entry from 1998. Julia was seven.

Today we set out on our big adventure to canoe around the Bowren Lakes for a week. The girls were excited and wanted to take along some good books for the long drive up north. I told them we'd stop at a bookstore and each of them could choose something to read. Lauren chose a George R.R. Martin book, and Marlise picked Dragonsong *by Anne McCaffrey. I took Julia over to the "young readers" section of the store and showed her various books I thought she might like to try. She has been making progress lately, but still reads very slowly. I picked out* Frog and Toad, *by Arnold Lobel — a book she always enjoyed when I read it out loud.*

"No," said Julia emphatically. "I want a big book."

She went over to the shelf filled with the Redwall series by Brian Jacques. Her cousin Meg has been devouring Redwall books for the past year. Julia chose the first book in the row.

"This one!" she said proudly. I hesitated. She'd never be able to read that! There weren't even any pictures — and it was about 120 pages long! I was worried she'd feel frustrated and defeated. I wanted her to pick something she could actually manage.

But she was determined that she was going to read Redwall. I bought the book. I was pretty sure she'd take one look at the dense print inside once we got settled in the car, and give up in discouragement. But I was totally surprised. Julia bent over her novel with a fierce look of determination. After we had been driving for about twenty minutes she suddenly looked up and announced, "I just read two pages!" A while later, she'd read two more. I can't figure out what, exactly, was going on in her head — she can't have been able to read more than half the words on the page. But she persisted stubbornly in poring over that Redwall book during the whole trip. By the time we got home, a week later, she was a reader.

When children are ready to tackle the skills necessary for a fulfilling adult life, they will tackle them with gusto. Julia was ripe for reading at the "normal" age of seven, but some children aren't ready or interested until much later. Two homelearning boys (from different families) I have watched grow up were both diagnosed as "dyslexic" at their different schools because they weren't reading by age eight. Rather than allow their sons to be labelled as disabled, the parents of these boys chose to pull them out of school and leave them free to learn at their own pace. Both boys didn't read until age twelve. But both, as it turns out, have become avid readers and writers. One has just finished an honours degree in political science; the other, although he has not chosen to go to university, is now a voracious reader who is astonishingly knowledgeable on a wide range of subjects.

What was all the fuss about? Why the urge to label children as "disabled" for following their own timetable instead of someone else's? Do educators actually believe that a healthy, intelligent human being, surrounded as we all are by books, newspapers, billboards, letters, email and bits of text wherever we look, will fail to learn to read? Apparently they do.

Children may not read when we think they should, but eventually they will want access to the shared cultural world just like everyone else. Apparently, almost all adults who "can't read" have been traumatized by school failure. The labelling and judgment they experienced as young children, and the resulting anxiety, is the cause of their disability — not any "wrong" wiring in their brains. According to literacy experts it takes only a few short hours of patient help and reassurance from a literate friend or volunteer to get these illiterate adults reading. Kids are no different. When they want to read (usually when they encounter something really *worth* reading, like Redwall for Julia), they will. Forcing them to read before they are ready is not only cruel but can ensure that in future they never discover the joy of books.

Gaining skill in writing is also, I have observed, a very natural and organic process. It goes hand in hand with reading. Lauren, Marlise and Julia liked to "write" at a very early age. They made squiggles and shapes on paper and then "read" to me what the squiggles meant. Sometimes I would let them dictate a story, which I would then type up and give back to them, leaving space for them to add their own illustrations. They were proud and amazed to see how their spoken words had turned into such crisp official-looking pages full of letters!

In time they began to write their own stories. I tried to refrain from correcting the spelling or grammar (which was especially hard when they were writing letters to their English-professor grandparents). Whenever I did interfere in their creative process with suggestions or corrections, it would take the wind out of their sails. Days would go by before they would take up the pen again. I would silently vow to keep my mouth shut next time.

When Marlise and Lauren were eight and ten years old I began to host a weekly creative writing group, attended by about ten homelearning children aged eight to fourteen. These writing sessions were wonderful. There were no rules or expectations, and no criticism or evaluation of the work done. We agreed not to comment on each other's spelling or grammar. Our role was simply to appreciate each other's creativity. I'd come up with some kind of writing exercise or game that all would do for thirty or forty minutes, and then we'd spend the rest of the time going around the table taking turns reading out loud what we had written. I always wrote and shared the exercise as well, because I didn't want to be the "teacher." I wanted to show the kids that adults could have fun creating too.

The children whose parents tended to correct them at home took longer to feel safe sharing what they had written. But after a few weeks, once they realized that no one was going to evaluate or judge what they had produced, even these hesitant children relaxed. In the end we all became quite prolific. The kids couldn't wait until their turn to read their story or poem out loud.

Once we'd moved to Mayne Island I began another writing group with homeschoolers in Victoria, which Julia also participated in for several years. (Since Victoria is the closest city to the island, we gradually shifted to using Victoria instead of Vancouver as our city-base for activities.) I think the writing clubs were inspiring for all who participated. The kids were always intrigued to see what the others in the room would come up with. They realized that there are an infinite number of ways to wreathe words together, none of them the "best" or "right" way, and that each of us possesses our very own boundless imagination. Several parents mentioned to me that their child's love of writing really took off as a result of the supportive atmosphere of the group. My philosophy was always that the point was to *write*, not to write "properly" or "well." The goal was expression. Creativity. And the bonus was that we all had so much fun sharing our creations with others. Skills would develop in their own sweet time. The important thing was to enjoy playing with words.

Gradually as the years went by, I noticed the girls' spelling improve. Their sentences became more fluent and complex, particularly as they started to read more challenging literature. What I value most is that now, as adults, they aren't afraid of writing, as so many people seem to be who suffered from being judged in school. *Fear of criticism kills creativity*. Reading and writing develop far better when young minds feel safe and unself-conscious than when they feel watched and evaluated by others.

What about math? I hear you ask. I have to answer, perhaps a little sheepishly, that not much formal training in mathematics occurred in our household. For sure the workbooks were hauled out now and then, usually after some well-meaning relative had warned the girls about the perils of being "dumb at numbers." Over the years I brought home various books that tried to make math seem fun and attractive. But the girls always balked. They just weren't willing to swallow learning as if it were some kind of preventive medicine, like a vitamin. Learning for them had to be useful and interesting.

What astounds me today is that, with very little formal training in math, the girls are able to get along just fine in the world. It makes me realize how permeated with numbers our daily lives are. Arithmetic, at least the basic operations of adding, subtracting, multiplying, dividing, handling fractions and percents etc., turns out to be as easy to pick up from life as reading and writing. Here is my journal entry from 1993. Marlise was six.

> *The other day Richard asked Marlise, "Have you been doing any numbers lately?"*
>
> *He's a little uneasy about my less-and-less structured approach to the kids' education. Marlise hadn't been working in her workbooks, but when we started to think back on all the figuring we'd been doing, there was a lot of number work! Marlise had been calculating the days until Halloween, subtracting the days, as each passed, from the total. She'd also been figuring out how old she'd be when, say, Julia was seven. That involves adding three years to whatever Julia's age would be. Same with Lauren's age and mine, and Richard's. Marlise loves to do this kind of calculation. She recently opened a bank account which now has $25 in it. She knows that each allowance will add $2 to her total. Yesterday she asked me to explain to her exactly how much a nickel, a dime and a quarter were worth. She*

*practised (on her own initiative) grouping coins together
and trying to figure out how much they added up to.*

As adults, Lauren, Marlise and Julia are able to earn and
handle money, to save and to budget for their various trips and
adventures. I have never heard any of them express a sense of being
math-deficient. They seem to have all the skill with numbers they
need to get by in the world.

Lauren, in fact, is turning out to have quite the head for
business. About five years ago, she and Blake founded Inkspoon,
a business specializing in handmade, wearable art. Lauren and
Blake create complex, thematic graphic designs that they silk-
screen onto sustainable-fibre, made-in-Canada clothing. They've
built a website where they post pictures of their current designs,
and are now making Internet sales all over North America.

For the past three years, Lauren has taken over doing the
books for Inkspoon. (Formerly they had hired one of their friends,
a commerce graduate.) Lauren is not afraid of math, nor is she
under the impression that she is in any way less capable with
numbers than the next person. She has a logical and systematic
mind and I have no doubt does a fine job as a bookkeeper. Her
grandmother, Kathryn, who died three years ago and who had
been an excellent bookkeeper all her life, would have been proud!

So again, after years of biting my nails, I am forced to come
to the conclusion that all the fuss about math in schools is a
tempest in a teapot. The level of numeracy that most of us need
in order to live functional lives is easily acquired. We do *not*
need algebra or calculus to get along in life; and to insist that
all students master these skills seems to me as cruel as requiring
that everyone, whether they are interested or not, play the violin
or study ballet. What a waste of energy and talent! The budding
astrophysicists among the nation's children will *demand* to learn
math, just as Marlise demanded to play the piano. When they ask
for it, let's give it to them. Otherwise, let them take what they
need and leave the rest.

What about applying to college when the time comes? If children don't have a high school diploma, how can they gain entrance to higher education? This problem turned out to be much easier for us to solve than we thought. Fortunately, the college system is not tied to the public school system. Most colleges welcome "mature" (over age nineteen) students who do not have a high school degree, and only require that they pass a test of language competency. My two younger daughters both began college at age eighteen, and gained entry by passing the Grade 12 English exam before applying to college. They simply registered, as homeschoolers, to sit the exam at a local high school. The whole procedure took two hours. Another home-schooled friend of ours went to college at seventeen and did so by taking the college's own language-proficiency test. I am pretty confident that any teenager who has spent time during adolescence reading books and engaging with the written word in some way or another will pass these tests.

I believe there are equivalent tests for math proficiency for those students wanting to enroll in the sciences. College admissions officers are generally very friendly and helpful, I have found. They know that young people who have learned outside of schools have an excellent reputation for being able students at the college level. Such students make self-directed and curious learners. Teachers are usually grateful to have them in class.

Designing a Life Worth Living

By Lauren Iredale

Insert 2

Occasionally I think back on my life so far and wonder at the chain of events and experiences that led to the path I am now taking. I am now twenty-seven years old. I live with my husband, Blake, on Salt Spring Island, in the partially completed house we have been building for the past two years. We own and operate a small clothing company called Inkspoon, which allows us to work from home and live a flexible and creatively rewarding lifestyle. We are currently expecting our first child. I am grateful that the work we have created for ourselves will allow us to be equal partners in parenting and give us the freedom to avoid any institutionalized care and schooling of our kids.

I was unschooled for most of my childhood until, at the age of sixteen, I chose to attend high school for grades eleven and twelve. After graduating, I enrolled at Emily Carr Institute of Art and Design. During my four years there, I studied all manner of art mediums, received a Bachelor of Media Arts degree, and also met my life partner, Blake. Ironically, the art medium essential to our livelihood now, silk-screening, was the one discipline that neither Blake nor I took any formal training in.

Throughout my teens and young adulthood I became increasingly aware that much is not right with the world. I began to learn how the effects of globalization and capitalism are destroying the quality of all life on this planet. The profit motive driving our society has forced most of us to work longer hours for lower pay and to consume increasingly toxic products and nutrient-deprived foods, and has had a catastrophic effect on the environment. I began to realize that these are just some of the negative results of a paradigm that values domination, competitive behaviour and the pursuit of profit above all else.

As I anticipate bringing a new life into this world, I am torn between dread about the future of our planet and a persistent hope that a sustainable, life-affirming way of life is possible.

I believe that individual creativity needs to become a cultural priority if we are to invent a new paradigm. But to do this we must recognize the environment that allows creativity to occur. I have often found that my best ideas come when my mind is relaxed and I'm free of self-consciousness and the awareness of time. I've had inspiration for poetry while sitting listening to music, for instance, or had a vision for a painting while I've been dancing. Sometimes my most seemingly "un-productive" behaviour gives rise to my best insights and inspirations.

As an unschooler — before I went to high school — I was allowed to decide how I spent my time. This gave me the freedom to listen to my intuition, to daydream and to pursue an interest until it no longer held charge. I think this ability to immerse myself in a field of exploration — whether it was drawing elves from a comic book, writing a novel, researching about horses or discussing the relationships between characters in a fantasy book with my mom — fostered my strength of focus and my confidence in my own ideas and creative abilities.

When I first started high school I remember the acute awareness of being "watched and timed." This feeling that my time was being monitored and judged was a creativity killer. Even when some aspect of the curriculum did catch my interest (a very rare occurrence), I was soon interrupted by the end of class time and forced to move on to something else.

This environment of being monitored also undermined my self-confidence. Knowing that my work was being judged and graded gave me a detached sense of seeing myself with two sets of eyes. Instead of immersing myself in the process of learning, I would be anticipating someone else's reaction to what I was doing. I know we cannot always escape the gaze of the world upon our actions and our work, and often we may request it. But I believe if we want to nurture our creativity we must give ourselves a space away from that judging gaze.

I think my desire to work for myself now that I am an adult, rather than be someone else's employee, stems from valuing the freedom I knew as an unschooler. I want to be able to honour my impulses and intuition moment to moment, and to engage in work that is close to my heart and that feels worthwhile to me. The feeling of being creatively engaged is, I think, essential for a fulfilling life. It may also be crucial to the question of our survival as a species.

Inkspoon, our clothing company, evolved out of a sense of play. While we were still at Emily Carr, Blake and I and a couple of good friends started experimenting after class with silk-screens. Our friend Basil was taking a course in silk-screening at UBC, and several times he snuck us into the studio after hours and gave us some basic tips on how to layer silk-screened prints onto clothes. We scrounged second-hand clothing items to print on from thrift stores, clothing swaps and friends' closets. Part of me wonders whether, if we had taken any formal training in the craft, we would still now be doing it. If we had been forced to learn "the rules" of silk-screening, and to have our work watched by an "expert," we might have felt too confined to continue finding any inspiration in it. The style of printing we have developed would probably shock most traditional silk-screeners. I think it is our innovative method, however, that gives our work such appeal.

Through trial and error, Blake and I have developed what we call our "freestyle" approach to silk-screening. We design our own graphics, make and expose our own screens and layer up prints upon a variety of fabrics in a unique way. Along with learning and perfecting this craft — with little or no expert guidance — we have had to learn how to run a business. This meant going up a steep and sometimes frightening learning curve. We've made lots of mistakes and had to learn from them.

Our goal has been to make the company as sustainable, ethical and environmentally friendly as possible. We have our clothes sewn up in small batches by a group of seamstresses in Vancouver and we hand-print them ourselves in limited edition runs in our home studio. Although outsourcing the work to companies overseas might make us more profitable, we know we would lose the quality and uniqueness that makes Inkspoon special. I think our own lifestyle would suffer too, if we gave up the pleasure and pride that comes from practicing our craft in favour of having a sweatshop full of employees.

The most artistic aspect of the business is the creation of new designs. In order to keep the process interesting to us, we are always endeavouring to come up with new ideas for print series. The themes of our designs tend to reflect our current interests, and have ranged from totemic animals, numerology, ancient cultures and sacred geometry to funk music, herbal medicine and the Occupy movement. I find the silk-screening process to be meditative and intuitive. While I work I listen to audio lectures, radio shows and books on tape; I enjoy this feeling of having both the intuitive and intellectual sides of my brain simultaneously engaged. Being my own boss means I also have the flexibility to build my work around my day rather than the other way around. If the sun comes out or a friend drops by for a visit I can stop what I'm doing to go for a walk or have tea.

Creativity is not just beautiful art or good ideas; it is also the ability to adapt to new circumstances and roll with change. I think the freedom to be my own authority while I was young has given me the confidence and resilience to deal with the ups and downs of running a small business. Blake and I have had to be willing to let go of expectations, and not be afraid to fail, in order to discover what works. It took us a few years to realize, for instance, that we were actually losing money by wholesaling to retailers. We discovered that we were much better off, and could make more money with less production, if we could eliminate the middle man and sell our clothes directly to customers. For the past few years we have managed this by touring the country selling at festivals and markets. This has been a fun adventure, but an exhausting way of earning a living in the long run. We are now focused on growing our web presence and selling online, and are currently shipping orders all over North America and even to Europe and Australia.

The creative process seems to require a balance of our inner and outer worlds. In order to make ourselves available to inspiration, to visions, we must free ourselves of the sense of being watched. We must let go of the culturally entrenched Judge who sits inside our minds. Once the spark of inspiration has ignited and we've manifested our idea we can then "test" our discovery by seeing how others respond to it.

At university I often found the critiques of my peers and teachers arbitrary and useless. But occasionally their reactions would help crystallize my ideas and let me know if what I was trying to say was being understood or not. Likewise, our Inkspoon Facebook page, where we can post pictures of our latest designs, allows us to get immediate reactions from hundreds of people. Some designs are far more popular than others. Some designs trigger negative reactions. When we create a design series that is really popular, we must decide whether to continue printing run after run of it, or remain true to our intention of making work that is one-of-a-kind as well as meaningful to ourselves. Ultimately Blake and I have to find our work interesting and inspiring. Sometimes that means moving on, even when we have a series that has proven to be a sure sell.

Growing up as an unschooler helped me trust my own inner voice and balance my inner and outer worlds. My goal now is to be receptive to the opinions of others while still remaining true to my authentic feeling of the world.

One of the underlying narratives of our current culture is that "success" in life is quantified by the amount of money you make. We don't tend to call into question how that money is made or at what cost. I think more and more people are waking up, however. More and more of us are starting to see the devastating effects of mass production, globalization and corporate greed. We are longing for a value system that puts sustainability and creativity first.

If we are going to become a more authentic and life-affirming culture we need a value system that measures success not by the size of one's bank account but by the satisfaction, enjoyment and feeling of connectedness a life holds. Blake and I have no desire to grow our company until it becomes the next Lululemon. Our aim instead is to create a lifestyle that lets us be free, self-determining, responsible citizens of this world. By living simply, and by working from home, we will be able to afford to raise our children in a way that helps them realize their own creative potential.

Perhaps one day we will develop schools or learning centres that encourage the individual creative force in each child to thrive. I believe that only by allowing the potential of each child to unfold in its own unique way can we hope to one day live in a flourishing society, one that is creatively diverse and productive, and yet is sustained by cooperation and by an inherent respect for all life. Although we may not be able to give this world to our children now, we can break our cultural trance of competition and hierarchy; we can allow our children to give themselves in love and strength to the world.

Chapter Nine
The Socialization Question

Compassion is not religious business, it is human business, it is not luxury, it is essential for our own peace and mental stability; it is essential for human survival.[23]

The Dalai Lama

Probably the most common question I have heard over the years is "but what about socialization?!" Schools, many people seem to assume, are where children learn to get along with other people. The playground roughhousing, the team sports, the classroom rivalry, the peer pecking-order, all serve, they believe, to develop children's ability to cope in the socially complex, competitive adult world. Children who miss out on school risk ending up socially backward. How will such children know how to mingle with strangers at cocktail parties, or hold their own at job interviews, or make jokes at board meetings, if they don't spend large chunks of their formative years with same-aged peers? Only in schools, these "socialization" advocates seem to assume, can we develop the social savvy necessary to succeed in life.

I agree that we are social animals. We need the company of other people in order to thrive, grow, learn and become fully ourselves. As soon as my children were born they sought out my face, anxious to interact with me. Current studies of babies suggest that the early mutual gazing of parent and child is crucial for the child's evolving sense of self. It's as if we need to see ourselves mirrored in the face of another to know that we are real. When a toddler stumbles and scrapes her knee, she immediately looks to her caregiver for an interpretation of what has just happened. A loving parent looks back with a sympathetic expression, mirroring the child's pain. The parent's mirroring soothes and reassures the child; it also helps her understand what she has just experienced. "Ouch, that hurts doesn't it? Here, we'll put a Band-Aid on it and it will feel better soon." The child feels safe inside the parent's response. The hurt knee is less painful and frightening when acknowledged by someone so deeply trusted.

Young children are curious about other people and continually seek social interaction. They also seek help interpreting the mysterious world unfolding around them. Whenever I took my young children with me to run errands I was always struck by what keen students of human nature they were. They studied everyone they encountered, from shopkeepers to nurses in the health clinic to the plumber fixing the toilet. They asked constant questions about human behaviour ("Why is that man waving a flag, Mommy?" "Why is she wearing those dark glasses?"). Everyone a child meets becomes a subject of investigation. And every person a child interacts with on a regular basis — parents, siblings, pets, grandparents, even the neighbour down the street — helps shape a child's emerging identity.

We become who we are through our relationships. We find out how other people work, and how we work, by interacting with the important people in our lives. Our sense of self depends on the image reflected back to us from the gaze of others.

This very fact should make us cautious. Young children are extremely impressionable and trusting. They have not yet developed defences against the cruelty of others. *We should be careful, therefore, not to expose children to harmful social situations from which they cannot escape.* Any social environment in which some are allowed to frighten, humiliate or bully others is dangerous to the emotional health of all involved. Toxic relationships are toxic for everyone, but for children most of all.

I think most people will admit that the "socialization" that goes on in schools is sometimes destructive rather than beneficial. When my nephew Adam was at school, he had a very hard time making friends. Something about Adam, whether it was his ponytail, or the cowboy hat he insisted on wearing, or his habit of speaking his mind, made the other boys in grade four tease him. On several occasions he was bullied and reduced to tears, and his crying only made the teasing worse. By grade six, Adam had come to view himself as an outsider who could not fit in. He took to spending time alone on the school playground rather than seeking out other children. We were all worried about him. No amount of coaching on how to get along with the other kids seemed to help. Adam felt thoroughly defeated by the social environment of school.

Luckily, his parents had the courage to let him drop out at age twelve and learn at home. It took several years for him gradually to shed the self-image of unpopular misfit that he had acquired at school, but he finally did. He began taking his fiddle to a regular Celtic music jam once a week in Victoria and found that the other musicians, all of whom were older, welcomed him into their midst. He connected with a couple of other unschooled boys who visited him on Mayne and joined him in making forts and building targets to shoot arrows at. He hung out with his cousins who accepted him as he was. Adam gradually stopped identifying himself as "weird."

This past summer, at the music festival he has created on Mayne Island, I watched Adam gracefully and masterfully organize a crew of about fifty volunteers as they built stages and outhouses, set up elaborate sound systems, cooked and served food, sold tickets, shuttled passengers and oversaw campers. I never saw Adam lose his temper. He was kind and appreciative and good-humoured with everyone he met. The Campbell Bay Music Fest is in its fifth year; its audience has grown from 100 or so to over 600. Since Adam himself has toured all over Canada with his band, Fish and Bird, he is well connected in the Canadian music scene. He has been able to persuade top-notch musicians to perform at the festival, despite the fact that he is not yet able to pay them very much. I would say the festival owes much of its success to Adam's social adeptness.

How did Adam become a gifted social animal? I believe that human beings are hard-wired for sociability. Allowed to grow and develop in a supportive and loving environment, we could all become talented at getting along with each other and skilled at knowing ourselves. Adam learned to love by being loved. He learned patience and tolerance by being with others who treated him patiently and tolerantly. He cultivated good humour by being among others who, rather than teasing and belittling him, were encouraging and supportive.

In order to become healthy social beings, children need the company of people with greater social awareness than themselves. They need to see kindness, cooperation and tolerance *modeled* in their daily lives. They need to be treated kindly so that they know how it feels. Empathy is a crucial human capacity. It is the source of our generosity, our talent for cooperation and intimacy and our willingness to share the world with others. A child's capacity for empathy grows and strengthens when her caregivers *empathize* with her. It shrivels when those around her ignore or thwart her feelings. We become as others treat us.

I do not believe that schools, as they are currently structured, foster kindness and tolerance, no matter what school motto hangs over the entrance. In schools, children spend their entire day confined with people their same age, people with the same undeveloped social ability. Where are the adults and older children capable of modeling how to communicate respectfully? Where are the empathetic mentors with honed skills at conflict resolution to remind ruffians on the playground, or gossips in the hallways, that it hurts to be ridiculed, and that there is room for everyone to take part?

There are the teachers and staff, of course, but the average school has an adult–child ratio of about 1:30. This is a new development in human evolution. Indigenous cultures do not segregate children from adults; instead, pre-industrial cultures the world over include children in the daily life of the community. Children become social beings by hanging out with people of all ages, by watching and helping the adults around them, and by participating in the rituals and ceremonies of their tribe. We, in contrast, seem to be asking children to *raise each other*. The "socialization" that too often goes on in schools isn't much different from what goes on in prisons: inmates either learn to "fit in" to the brutal, hierarchical prison culture, or they are crushed.

Children are naturally attracted to each other. They love chances to play together. But not all day, every day. Children need alone time. They also need social diversity, people of all ages to hang out with and learn from. I think it's time for the tables to be turned. It's time for schools to be called to account. They should be asked to look closely at the kind of socializing that goes on within their walls and on their playing fields. "What about socialization?!" should be asked of schools by parents who want their kids to grow up kind. Children need relationships, but they need good ones. They need loving connections if they are to grow up capable of love.

Chapter Ten
Our Year in Sports

Throughout life, from school until we die, we are taught to compare ourselves with another; yet when I compare myself with another I am destroying myself.[24]

Jiddu Krishnamurti

After we pulled Lauren out of school, I felt uneasy being different from the other families on our block. One solution, I thought, was to encourage the girls to get involved in team sports. That way they could have something in common with their neighbourhood friends. It was my way of saying, "See, our girls aren't completely isolated and weird. They are still able to play ball at the park with the other children!"

We were still living in Vancouver at the time. I signed up with another mother to co-coach a softball team for girls Lauren's age, and Richard coached a five-pitch baseball team for six- and seven-year-old boys and girls that Marlise joined. We started out the season with new running shoes and high hopes.

Marianne, the neighbourhood mother who coached with me, believed like I did that the important thing was for the kids to have *fun*. We kept practices light and relaxed. We joked and goofed around a lot. We let all the girls take turns playing the various positions rather than trying to figure out who was the "best" at certain skills.

Then came the games. The parents would show up and start shouting and cheering and advising from the sidelines — and the sense of playful ease would evaporate. I would notice a kind of tension settle into the girls' faces. Those who were not strong players would look anxious and miserable, fearful of being humiliated in front of their peers and their families, and those who were athletic would acquire a grim, determined, "make or break" set of the jaw. These were nine-year-olds! And what was worst of all, I would notice an anxiety arise in myself. I felt a need to prove to these parents that I was a good-enough coach; that I, too, could inspire a winning team.

My moment of truth came one day towards the end of the season, when we were up against the "best" team in the league. The girls were nervous. By this point in their young lives, they had thoroughly internalized the assumption that it was much better to win than to lose. They didn't relish the idea of being, as they called it, "creamed."

Here is my journal entry from that day in March 1994:

What an awful day. We were slated to play the Wildcats — supposedly the best team in the league. The girls were nervous. Marianne and I were nervous too. But we tried to be cheerful, and reminded the girls, "Just have fun. Remember it's only a game!"

Well, when the Wildcats showed up, even Marianne and I started to quake in our running shoes. The coach was a muscular, unsmiling middle-aged man with the jaw of an ex-army sergeant. He barked commands and his team of girls, all with tight ponytails, very clean t-shirts, and strangely vacant expressions on their faces, leapt into action. They spaced out in pairs on the playing field and proceeded to "warm up," firing the softball back and forth with astonishing precision. It was softball boot camp. Marianne stood with her mouth open, gawking. I glanced across at Lauren's appalled face and my heart sank.

When it was time to start the game, the Wildcats fell neatly into line and marched up to form a tight circle around their coach. "Now team!" he called out in a martial tone. "Remember what I said. If you're not winners, what are you?" "Losers!" the girls all shouted as one. "Right!" yelled the coach. "And what are we?" "Winners!" they shouted again. They put their fists together in a final cheer. None of them were smiling.

I couldn't believe my eyes and ears. And of course, we were walloped. Our girls played worse than they ever had. It seemed the more they began to lose, the more they seemed to forget everything they had ever learned about playing softball. Their mood entirely affected their performance. It didn't help that the ten or so parents from our team that had shown up to watch kept shouting instructions at the girls. One dad kept hollering, "Just focus, girls! Focus!" As if that was going to help!

Then it came to the closing ritual of every game, when the two teams line up and shake hands with each other, all the while intoning the words "good game, good game." I felt nearly sick. Why should our girls have to call it a "good game" when it evidently had not been a good one? I suddenly felt as though I was watching a kind of macabre initiation rite: these young girls were all being inducted into our cultural Religion of Competition.

When the other coach came up to shake hands with me after the game he offered me some (unasked for) advice. "You should work on attitude. *Skills too — gotta drill those skills. But in the end, it's all in the attitude." His grip was vice-like and his face hard-edged and unanimated, like a mask.*

"Yeah," I muttered, "I'll remember that."

Needless to say, I didn't sign up to coach another season. Our match with the Wildcats caused some scales to fall from my eyes. I saw that the world of organized sport is actually the same world as that of compulsory schooling. They are two sides of the same coin.

George Sage, a sociologist who writes extensively about the role of sports in contemporary society, thinks competitive sports condition kids to being cogs in an impersonal bureaucracy. "Organized sport," he writes, "from youth programs to the pros, has nothing at all to do with playfulness — fun, joy, self-satisfaction — but is, instead, a social agent for the deliberate socialization of people into the acceptance of the prevailing social structure and their fate as workers within bureaucratic organizations."[25]

Alfie Kohn explores this idea further in his book *No Contest: The Case Against Competition*. Throughout the book, Kohn reviews hundreds of studies from the social sciences that contradict our society's assumption that competition is necessary for a healthy society. Speaking of competitive sports, he writes:

> *Sport does not simply build character; it builds the kind of character that is most useful for the social system. From the perspective of our social (and economic) system . . . it is useful to have people regard each other as rivals. Sports serve the purpose nicely, and athletes are quite deliberately led to accept the value and naturalness of an adversarial relationship in place of solidarity and collective effort. If he is in a team sport, the athlete comes to see cooperation only as a means to victory, to see hostility and even aggression as legitimate, to accept conformity and authoritarianism. Participation in sports amounts to a kind of apprenticeship for life in contemporary America, or, as David Riesman put it, 'the road to the boardroom leads through the locker room.'* [26]

Although coaches and educators tell us "the game is the thing" or "the point is to participate," I am deeply suspicious of their motives. The system is set up to keep everyone's eyes on the prize. Who beat whom? Who got the medals? Who made it on the honour roll? These are the questions people in a competitive environment ask, because a competitive environment makes us feel anxious and unsafe. As Kohn points out, "to structure an event as a competition is . . . first and foremost to designate a goal: victory." And victory by definition requires a defeat. People at constant risk of defeat — constantly anxious, in other words — are useful. They try harder to please those who hand out the prizes.

The tragedy of a competitive system is that, ultimately, most people get excluded from the game. In the words of John Holt:

> *Everything in our traditional system of athletics is a* weeding out, *a cutting away of people until there is only one left . . . In the athletic program of most schools we start off at first-grade level with 1,500 runners, players, participants. Not one child out of a hundred, at age six, would rather watch a game than take part in it. By the end of high school we may have at most 100 participants. The other 1,400 are sitting up there in the stands, watching them — maybe cheering now and then. Our so-called competitive athletic programs are perfect for turning participants into watchers, doers into consumers, runners into sitters.* [27]

Obviously the "point" of our current system is *not*, as coaches and sports enthusiasts would like us to believe, "to participate." The point is to win. And in a win/lose situation most people eventually won't feel safe enough to join in.

My daughter Marlise, who was over in another part of the park playing five-pitch while Lauren was losing to the Wildcats, made a poignant remark after one game that showed how far her young heart was from "accept[ing] the value and naturalness of adversarial relationships." Her comment has stuck with me to this day. She was six at the time. Her team had lost many games in a row, but this night they had a victory. When Marlise found out they had won she jumped up and down and screamed delightedly along with her teammates. "We won! We won!" they all squealed. Then Marlise looked across at the members of the other team. Their little heads hung and they scuffed their feet dejectedly in the sand of the baseball diamond. This team had lost every single game they had played that season. Marlise's sensitive face immediately fell. She looked up at me and said in a small voice, "Mommy, I like it best when *both* teams win."

Why *can't* both teams win? Who does it serve to have children (or adults for that matter) pitted against one another? Perhaps Sage and Kohn are right. Sport is just another arena in which we are told to accept unquestioningly that there have to be winners and losers. Some are entitled to the good things in life and others are not. Those with the right "attitude" — who play by the rules and win — are rewarded with wealth and power. The poor and disempowered, the losers of life's competition, are supposed to be "good sports" and put up with it.

That was our last year of team sports. Of course, if the girls had clamoured to play, we would not have forbidden them. But I sure wasn't going to participate in that world any longer. I had seen the dark face of competition and was repelled. Did I really want to encourage my children to regard others as "rivals"? Or did I want to nurture and protect the deep, spontaneous compassion that Marlise felt towards the members of the opposite team, her desire to see them happy too? Maybe there is a way to rescue team sports from the "attitude" that currently pervades it, but I myself can't see how. Our family went back to walking, running, cycling, horseback riding, swimming, climbing, swinging and building forts — activities in which there is room for everyone to be a winner.

Chapter Eleven
Journaling: A Tool for Self-Discovery

Nothing in life is to be feared. It is only to be understood.[28]

Marie Curie

One of the most important educational tools in our household was the journal. We gave our children blank books to write in, even before they knew how to write. I myself kept a journal, so they often saw me sitting with pen in hand. They grew up believing that writing down one's experiences, thoughts, impressions, questions, worries and dreams was as normal a human activity as brushing one's teeth. Over the years of keeping journals their skills at writing developed dramatically. But most importantly, they learned to know themselves.

I suspect that self-awareness is essential for intimacy. We have to first know how we feel before we can put ourselves in another's place. Journaling helps us develop the habit of self-reflection and self-awareness. Journaling is a practice of conversing with oneself, of exploring, examining and reflecting on one's experiences as they arise. Often over the years I have sat down to write in my journal with a vague feeling of anxiety or sadness or unease, not knowing quite what the problem was. As I begin to write, whatever has been bothering me starts to come clear. "Ah, so *that's* it!" The simple act of awareness causes whatever anxiety or heaviness I am feeling to lighten a little and grow less threatening.

Here is an excerpt from Marlise's journal at age eleven. At that point we had been living on Mayne Island for over a year and were still raising lambs for slaughter. The girls and I were vegetarians, but the rest of our extended family loved eating lamb. I had explained to the girls why it was important to keep the sheep on the fields. We needed to raise some sort of food crop in order to have status as a farm and keep the property taxes affordable. Raising lambs provided the farm with an income and also kept the pastures around our house grazed and beautiful. Otherwise, they would soon be filled with scotch broom and blackberry vines. The girls and I all loved being shepherds. We loved the daily chore of feeding the sheep and the yearly lambing season with its drama of birth and death. None of us, however, enjoyed the inevitable moment when it came time to ship the lambs off to the butcher; then there were lots of tears and questions!

In this journal entry Marlise is processing her feeling of rage and powerlessness at what she felt was the crime of allowing our lambs to be killed. I've corrected the spelling, but left the punctuation as she wrote it. Ken was a neighbour who had been teaching us about raising sheep.

> *Right now Ken and my parents are talking about the lambs and how much they can get for them. No one seems to care as much as I do! I love my lambs. I've watched them grow. When people talk about killing animals and eating them I just get sick! I can't stand it! Lauren and Mom don't really care! They've gotten too tough. I wish I could take all the lambs and run away to a deserted island where there are no people!*
>
> *I'm not going to write capital letters at the beginning of a meat-eater's name. They are too low. They are the lowest animal in the world! Why can't they just eat like the civilized vegans? There are NO answers to any questions. Absolutely NOT. NO. NOT ONE. NUTS! I'm going to*

go and hide in my little hole away from this pathetic little meager planet with its little creatures trying to survive by killing and torture.

That was an interesting little spasm I just went through. But it's true I hate meat eaters. But I love them. I can't help it they're family. Does that mean I hate my Dad. True? Of course true. No… of course not. NUTS!

What I love about this portrait of Marlise's eleven-year-old mind is that you see her struggling passionately with some of the moral "grey areas" that we continually encounter in life. She is learning that "right" and "wrong" are complex, that relationships involve tolerance and forgiveness. She is also learning about herself. If she had not been able to vent her powerful feelings in a private journal she may not have had the opportunity to process her anger and come to some kind of acceptance of the situation.

Journals should be places of complete freedom that no one else gets to look at unless invited, and where no worry about "correct" spelling or grammar cramps the creative flow. When the girls were younger, the pages of their journals often contained just a few letters or numbers and many drawings. Gradually, more and more text filled the pages. The content of the journals shifted dramatically as the girls matured. Before the age of eleven or twelve, they wrote mainly about external events. With the onset of puberty, their journals became places where they could explore dark thoughts and feelings.

Adolescence is a challenging time for human beings. When I began researching this book, Julia allowed me to read some of her old journals, which she had kept very private throughout her teens. Here is a journal entry of Julia's at age thirteen:

I try not to restrain myself, but I do not know how. I feel like I am restrained. Maybe it is fear. Maybe I'm just scared. But there seems to be something lurking. That I cannot get my mind past. I am clumsy in my ways. Clumsy. Shadow not my mind's work. Shadow nothing else. Shadow only what you need shadowed. So you see, so you see. I'm forgetting my restraint. I am losing all my consciousness. And falling far away in this wide open space. This field of cloudy grey has many choices. But it's still blackened by the lurking of . . . what? Shadows in the lock. Forgiving nothing, seeking something. Alone I stand. Remote. Until light shines from deep dark spaces. Closing out loneliness and beauty. Forgetting sense. Feel the summer wind through grasses both dry and tall. Shriveled by days and brightness. Hot. Sanctuary and tide pool and sun. The sun in the solar system deep in the galaxy surrounded by many many cold staring stars. Burning universes. Lifeless, loveless fire. Beauty resists temptation. Forgiving nothing. Finding something. Sun stares. Sharp, dark juices sucked from the very earth itself. Still and unforgiving. I stand alone.

In this journal passage I recognize myself at a similar age: for the sensitive adolescent the world seems to break into fragments, the comfortable truths of childhood crumble, revealing the "deep, dark spaces" of one's own vast depths. The ground beneath one's feet feels shaky and uncertain. The sky overhead reveals "burning universes" that are both threatening and alluring. The Self becomes aware of its own existence for the first time, sensing its limitation — its "restraint" — as well as its fundamental aloneness. One becomes aware of having "many choices," but the burden of freedom can be painful and confusing.

At puberty all three of my daughters wrote pages and pages of this kind of intense introspective writing. I would notice that whenever they were upset or had suffered a disappointment or frustration they would head directly for their room and their journals. Journaling became for them both a therapeutic exercise, helping them restore inner equilibrium after an intense emotional experience, and a method of self-discovery. It was also one of the ways they developed their capacity to empathize. Knowing ourselves helps us know each other.

Chapter Twelve
Ordinary Genius

Everybody is a genius. But if you judge a fish by its ability to climb a tree, it will spend its whole life believing that it is stupid.[29]

Albert Einstein

When I first told my friend Tamsin, a fellow unschooling mother, that I planned to write this book she said, "Please talk about raising ordinary people! All the books I read when we first started out were about families whose kids were off to Harvard or were virtuoso musicians or math whizzes. When I took my son out of school it wasn't so he could become some kind of prodigy. It was so that he could be happier being himself."

I, too, took Lauren out of school simply so that she could be happier. I wasn't one of those "stage moms" desperate to raise a star. I didn't expect to turn my daughters into geniuses. But the strange thing about unschooling is that it tends to allow children to develop in extraordinary ways.

Tamsin's own three children are a case in point. Her oldest son, at twenty-three, is studying literature and biology in college. He is also a champion fencer who aspires to compete in the Olympics. Her daughter was accepted into the Victoria College of Art at the age of fifteen because her skills at drawing and painting were already so highly developed. The youngest was a talented and sought-after hockey goalie until, in his early teens, he suffered an injury and had to quit. I am sure he will soon be diving into some new pursuit with the same passion and dedication he brought to his hockey playing.

Children who don't go to school have one thing their schooled peers don't have: *time.* They have lots and lots of relaxed, unpressured time to pursue their interests and curiosities. And as anyone who has become proficient at anything will tell you, time is what it takes to become skilled. I once overheard an admiring audience member ask my unschooled nephew Adam after a concert how he had become so good at the fiddle. "Twelve years," was Adam's answer. "It takes at least twelve years of playing every day. That's the only way to get good." Adam was twenty-one at the time. He had been playing the fiddle with wholehearted persistence since the age of nine.

Genius is the result of going deep rather than skimming along the surface of an activity. Becoming excellent at anything requires, as Richard often says, "attention times time." Studies of how the brain learns seem to indicate that it creates "maps" in order to perform tasks. Any activity we engage in over and over, with a great deal of focus and attention, will cause the brain to create a "map" of that activity. No matter what the activity is — whether it is playing the piano or solving advanced calculus equations or coordinating the physical movements necessary to be a top-notch swing dancer — once we have a thorough mental map the skill becomes easier and easier to perform. In fact, the brain actually changes, structurally, in response to repeated demands to develop certain abilities. The brain of a musician, for instance, looks different than that of someone not musically inclined. The area of the cerebral cortex most involved in music is much larger in the pianist than in, say, a writer or a gardener.

Deep, focused attention changes the brain, which in turn enables even greater depths of focus and learning. Genius, you might say, feeds on itself. It starts as an impulse or inclination and becomes in time a powerful developmental influence. We are literally shaped by our passions.

There is another key ingredient of genius: the ability to think outside the box. Sir Ken Robinson, in his famous 2006 TED Talk on Education, called it "divergent thinking." "Divergent thinking," he explains, "is the ability to see lots of possible answers to a question, lots of possible ways to interpret a question, to think laterally, to think not just in linear or convergent ways, to see multiple answers, not one." Robinson argues that 98 percent of children at age five test at genius level for divergent thinking. By adulthood, this percentage has dropped to 2 percent. What has happened in the interim? Robinson blames school. "We don't grow into creativity," he says, "we grow out of it. Or rather, we get educated out of it."[30]

In the environment of school, children have little opportunity either to go deep, or to think divergently. There is too often a "right" answer to the teacher's question, one that shuts off further questions and explorations. Moreover, in the classroom, a child rarely has a chance to engage with any activity or idea for long. Bells ring. Subjects change. Conversations are continually cut short. Though students are exposed to new things, any given area of curiosity is rarely allowed enough mental space to make a lasting impression. After twelve years of this enforced "attention deficit disorder," students often no longer remember what it feels like to be intellectually or imaginatively absorbed. They have lost the habit of being deeply engrossed by their experience and can only hold a train of thought for a short while. Genius has a hard time thriving under such conditions.

I love the fact that there are an infinite number of ways for human beings to be smart. One unschooled lad I know can fix almost any machine he encounters. He has a "genius" for mechanics, although he has had no formal training whatsoever. Another young man is an amazing cook. He reads recipe books for fun, and loves to experiment with new combinations of flavours. His palate is so finely developed he can tell you all the ingredients in a sauce just by tasting it.

Young people can turn their attention to almost anything, from cars to stars, from social activism to farming to philosophy.

Some children find early on a single focus for their passion and curiosity; others move through many stages of interest and develop several areas of expertise rather than a single one. They may occasionally need help gaining access to tools — to bicycles or books, to shovels or telescopes, for instance. But mostly they need us to *trust* that they will discover, in their own time and in their own way, the natural talent waiting to unfold within them.

What if, as Einstein says, "everybody is a genius"? What if all of us, given the right supportive, relaxed and loving environment, are capable of becoming excellent at what we love? Imagine living in a world peopled by geniuses — how vibrant and rich life would be!

I consider my children to be geniuses. Their creativity and capacity for innovation constantly astonishes me. All three are artists. All three also have strong leadership qualities. Lauren is a designer, writer and entrepreneur with an inventive mind and a talent for organizing — for the past two years she has managed to run a successful home-based business while living in a construction site! Marlise is a prolific composer and performer and such a compassionate listener that many of her friends come to her for counseling. Julia's paintings and drawings are arrestingly unique and emotionally powerful. Sometimes when I see some new image she has created I can't help asking, "Wherever did you get that idea from?" I am continually amazed by her originality.

My daughters' genius is not special or unusual. *We all have it.* It is the ordinary creativity and aliveness that dwells in every one of us, but which has too often been stifled by conventional schooling.

Robinson says, "You cannot predict the outcome of human development. All you can do is like a farmer create the conditions under which it will begin to flourish." Growing ordinary geniuses requires a special setting. In order to nurture excellence in our children we need to provide lots of fresh air and sunlight. We need to protect the tender shoots of enthusiasm and curiosity as they appear, and to resist any temptation to prune a child's passion through judging and coercion. And we'd better stop trying to make fish climb trees! When we label some interests or skills as more useful or worthy than others, and then force all children to aspire to only those, we waste so much human potential. Genius covers a vast range. Each of us has unique and wonderful gifts to share with the world if given a chance.

Chapter Thirteen
Fallow Times

The way up and the way down are one and the same.[31]

Heraclitus of Ephesus

Sometimes things don't go very well. Life leaves an acrid taste in the mouth. Your children don't seem to be thriving. Rather than the hotbed of creativity and enthusiasm you had hoped for, the family home has turned into a scene of squabbling and whining. Your way of life appears to be one big mistake.

Here is my journal entry from the fall of 1995:

Today everyone is bored and grumpy. It's been raining all week so we are stuck indoors. The house is a mess. I don't have the energy or heart to clean up. The kids are no help either. They just want to hang on me and pick fights with each other all day long.

If any of my neighbours looked in through the windows right now, they would be appalled. They would probably want to call Social Services and report that our home-schooling life is seriously damaging my kids!

Sigh. These times are the "dark nights of the soul" for me. They test my faith, both in the kids and in myself. I have to remember to keep breathing. I have to remind myself to be grateful for the many wonderful moments that do *come along, and not to fret too much over the difficult patches . . .*

No life is without its ups and downs. Human beings just aren't capable of feeling perpetually positive about existence. Moods come and go, energy levels rise and fall. Some days the sky is oppressively overcast. Other days the sun streams through the windows and makes us happy to be alive. There are periods when our relationships are light and harmonious, others when they seem fraught with conflict.

When we feel discouraged we tend to look for someone to blame. Often we blame ourselves. We think we should fix what's wrong by changing course and starting all over again. Homelearning parents are perhaps especially prone to self-doubt. When our kids aren't thriving, we wish, like other parents, that we could blame the "system." But that's not an option for us. Since we have chosen to go our own way, we are stuck with full responsibility for our choices.

Occasionally things really are so bad that we need to take immediate action. But over the years I have found that often if we just relax and trust that "this too shall pass," things improve on their own. Life is a sweet and sour mix. The trick is to get through the tough times as best we can, and be ready to savour the wonderful times when they arrive. And sometimes a seemingly dark or painful episode turns out to be a gift in disguise.

Boredom, I have found, is often such a gift. Nothing seems to put parents into a panic more than the thought that their child is "bored." Boredom is a downright dirty word in our culture. If you feel "bored," there must be something wrong with you, or with your life, or with your relationships.

Watching my children grow has shown me, however, that periods of boredom or "fallowness" aren't just painful stages that must be stoically endured. They are in fact necessary phases of growth; what appears to be boredom is actually an interior process of incubation and evolution that will eventually lead to a surge of creativity.

Here is another excerpt from my journal:

August 1995

For the past few days Marlise has complained of having nothing to do. Today she and Lauren are deeply engrossed in playing with paper people they've cut out and coloured in. They've made them furniture — beds, tables, even a toilet and a bathtub! All their own idea and very elaborate. Marlise is keeping notes on a pad of paper about the people they've invented: their names and attributes, their interests, who they are related to, etc. The girls have been at it for hours.

Julia, at four, doesn't yet have the concentration span to play along. Instead, she is padding around the cabin, or sitting in a chair singing to herself, or climbing into my lap and saying, "Mommy, I love you!"

Just now I had a surge of anxiety about her. Is she bored? She has no one to play with and today hasn't found anything that captures her interest.

But then I remind myself that she has had so many vivid experiences lately, like yesterday morning going down to the beach and clambering over the sandstone rocks to the "seal caves," or earlier in the week exploring the tide pools by the lighthouse, or finding the huge dead seal that had washed up on the beach, or last night sitting around the fire with the coal oil lanterns lit. She needs some quiet, unscheduled, unstimulating time to digest all the new things she is learning about the world.

Hmmm. Even as I've been sitting here writing, Julia has passed through a phase of restlessness and is suddenly now intensely focused. She found a pen and her "journal" and has come to sit beside me at the table. She asked me to show her how to write the word "hi," which she then practised several times. Now she is drawing more squiggles and asking me what letters they make. Now she's trying numbers. Now she is practising writing her name. How busy and intent and happy she is all of a sudden!

I, too, go through periods where I just can't seem to get anything done. There are days when I want to sit down and write or compose music and instead I find myself wandering around the house, puttering at chores, staring out the window, making yet another cup of tea. I just can't seem to settle down and focus on a task. It's as if my life force is occupied elsewhere.

I have learned from observing myself and my children that what seems like boredom may actually be something else. We may just be exhausted. Maybe life has been intense and stimulating lately and our emotional batteries need time to recharge. We might also be distracted by an inner process of grieving. Perhaps we have suffered some blow to our sense of well-being, some loss or disappointment or hurt. A cruel comment, for instance, or an embarrassing failure, has taken its emotional toll. We may not even be consciously aware that we are in pain; life just doesn't seem very appealing at the moment.

Sometimes apparent boredom is not masking either exhaustion or pain. Sometimes we are in a state of incubation. Though nothing on the surface seems to be happening, the unconscious mind is hard at work. Deep within, things are stirring, shifting, evolving and recombining. The creative process is underway.

A friend once asked about our lifestyle, "However do the children fill their day?" The truth is, sometimes the girls weren't able to fill their day at all. Sometimes one or the other of them appeared to drift in the doldrums. Interests that once gripped her imagination had lost their appeal. She couldn't seem to turn her attention to anything for long, but would flit listlessly from one activity to another. Or sit staring out the window for hours on end. This fallow period could last for days or weeks or even months.

At such times, it was hard for me to resist the desire to rush in and fix things. At times I desperately wanted to end my child's discomfort (and by extension, my own) by finding something for her to do. But when I was able to take some deep breaths and patiently observe, rather than intervene, in the process unfolding before me, I was often pleasantly surprised. Eventually the restlessness would shift. The fallow period would come to an abrupt end, unleashing a storm of creativity. Lauren at age fifteen, for instance, after a month or two of restlessness threw herself into the writing of a very long and complex fantasy novel. She worked with astonishing single-mindedness and dedication, sitting at her desk in her room for four or five hours a day for several months until the first draft was finished. Her ability to focus so intently on a single task astonished me.

Boredom is like sinking down into a deep inner well. It's an uncomfortable, disorienting feeling at first. But when finally you reach the bottom, arriving at the cool, rejuvenating depths of your inner life, you begin to surface again. You bring with you something new: a treasure from below.

The trick with fallow times is to be patient. Whether we are healing, recharging or incubating something new, we need the chance to be vacant for a while. Though it's hard to stay open to lassitude when it comes, we should try. If we can learn to surrender to that empty, aimless feeling, rather than labelling it "lazy," we will eventually see a shift. After all, the only constant is change. We are never *stuck* anywhere — not even in the doldrums. Instead, we are always evolving. Fearing boredom is like fearing ourselves, fearing our own rich, mysterious and transformative depths.

It could be that children today who have their days filled for them by school, after-school classes, play-dates and homework are not given enough chances to develop their creativity. They are not allowed to be fallow. I also suspect that children who have been kept busy during their childhoods will seek such compulsive busy-ness throughout their lives. They won't know how to be still and wait, and so will miss out on the bounty of a creative inner life. Avoiding boredom at all costs means avoiding an encounter with oneself.

One of the greatest gifts that parents can pass on to their children is a basic, fundamental faith in the processes of life. Existence is mysterious. Energy ebbs and flows; optimism and curiosity wax and wane. But *through all the ups and downs growth is always occurring*. Creative impulses, like seeds, often germinate in the dark. If we can stay patient and accepting of the difficult phases of our lives we might end up quite surprised by the gifts they bring. Sometimes the way down is the way up.

The Unhurried Mind

By Marlise Iredale

Many months ago my mom asked me to write an article for her book, and at first I was excited to share my perspective with all of you. But as my life filled up, the excitement passed, and this article soon turned into just another stressful thing that I had to get done. Plus, since I have a large appetite for life (as my mother likes to say) and am prone to distraction, countless things have gotten in the way of my completing this beast. At first I was touring with my band, and any free time we had between performances and driving I was much more inclined to spend meditating or unwinding my tension-filled body in the woods. After that I was interrupted by a soul-calling to travel alone to Indonesia for a couple of months. Now I am home again, recording an album with my band, and as I sit down to write, I notice my body and mind are overfull with so many ever-changing inspirations and convictions that I struggle to find one point of view to write from. There is too much activity in my mind, not enough space. Instead of writing, I stray from my desk to tinkle on the piano, or to spin my fire staff in the field to try to become good enough to join the circus, or to plan my next bold move either as an expressive arts therapist, a travelling vagabond clowning through Europe or a serious student at the Berklee School of Music in Boston, finally fulfilling my potential as a one-woman musical extravaganza! Oh yeah, the article.

Is my distractibility a result of not being properly educated in the school system to do things I don't particularly want to do? Is the fact that I am so committed to following what is alive inside of me in the moment a positive quality or have I just not developed a proper work ethic? Many questions gurgle up inside of me, making it very difficult to choose any sort of position to write from. Is this supposed to be another homelearner success story about how I "turned out well" and everyone can relax now because the experiment worked? But what if I didn't actually turn out well at all? Have I even finished turning? I am twenty-five years old, so that means I must have finally turned into *something*? Oh god, what if it actually isn't any good at all, this thing I've turned into?

I guess my parents can tell people that I seem to have turned into something that is continuously unfolding and changing, which is either wonderful or horrifying depending on your outlook. The real question is, what does it mean to grow into a "successful" person? Does it mean being able to make a lot of money? Or does it mean to be able to live an authentic, un-predictable, at-times-confusing, at-times-marvelous human life?

To unschool, or to lifelearn, is to completely re-evaluate what it means to live a meaningful life. The emphasis is placed on who we *are*, not on what we *do*. I feel that my parents are proud of me not because I have "amounted to much" in the eyes of society, but because I am connected to who I am and what I care about. I am very aware of what is alive inside of me and am committed to following it down whatever path it takes me. I am also aware that I need space in order to discover myself, and that I don't always give myself the space I need. The periods of my life that I have spent engaged in relentless activity and in the constant company of others have often left me feeling confused and disconnected from my centre. Although my parents have always encouraged me to follow my bliss, I am not immune to society's persuasive beliefs. Our culture's predominant value of "getting busy accomplishing things no matter what" has had its effect on me.

I love to work hard at something I'm passionate about, but I find our culture's productivity obsession to be more of a masochistic kind, a fixation on busy-ness just for busy-ness's sake. This was emphasized to me the other day when an older friend passed me on the street and said "Hey Marly, how's it going? Keepin' busy?" He was so busy himself that before I even had a chance to answer he continued, "Good to hear, keep it up!" and kept on walking! Until then I had never fully noticed how ridiculous this greeting is. It didn't seem to matter what I was busy with, as long as I was busy with something.

I grew up exposed to two very different worlds: my mom's free-flowing lifestyle with us at home and my dad's highly goal-oriented lifestyle at work. My father, as most other dads I knew growing up, felt pressure to be a big provider for his family. He was very influenced by the productivity demands of our society and fully participated in the busy-ness game. Although I knew he was passionate about his work, I could also sense the effect his stressful lifestyle was having on his emotional and spiritual well-being. He was strung out and stressed a lot of the time. I could also sense his occasional worry that we weren't being more productive at home.

When I was about ten years old my father came home from work one day appearing very depleted and unhappy. I remember the strained, weary look on his still-young face as he sat across from me at the dinner table. He told me he had three kinds of days: OK days, shitty days and *really* shitty days. I felt so sad for him. I also felt a little guilty that we were having such a fun time at home while he was slaving away at work. I could see that in order for my mom to have the space and time to stay home with us, he had to spend the majority of his life in a stressful work environment. In some ways, he was our freedom's sacrifice. I saw this in other homeschooling families. Usually the mom stayed home full-time with the kids while the dad worked full-time. The fathers I knew all had a certain drained quality to them. To me, it didn't seem like a very good arrangement. I hoped that when I grew up and had a family there could be another way for us to live.

From what I have seen in others and have experienced in myself, this frantic drive towards activity stems from a deep-seated feeling of inadequacy. I have heard that when the Dalai Lama first came to North America he had to have the term "low self-esteem" explained to him. He was puzzled by it. His people do not struggle with the same sense of self-loathing that seems to be enfolded into the very fabric of western society. Where does this insecurity come from? From advertising? From religion? From a deep disconnection from our bodies and from the earth?

Our cultural system relies on the ever-increasing production and consumption of stuff. To keep the system growing, we have to use up more and more of the planet's resources. Exploitation, social inequality and mass environmental devastation are the result. And in order to keep the wheels of this big machine turning — in order for us to constantly work to produce and consume commodities that are not essential to our survival or well-being — we must believe that we are not "enough" if we don't.

The school system aims to prepare children for this society. Does it do this by ensuring they grow up to feel bad about themselves? Or is our culture's pervasive feeling of inadequacy so strong that it is impossible to avoid it, in school or out?

When I was a kid there was such a feeling of expansiveness to life. The days were not compartmentalized into hours and minutes, filled with tasks and goals. The moments seemed to stretch on forever. The hours hovered suspended, like the endless unfurling of a cloudless summer sky. I could sink into an imagination game or an art piece for eternities, unhurried by the awareness of time passing. There was no thinking about past or future, there was only the moment and the game and my little heart filled by an open world. In the openness of that world I was a simple human child, an animal connected to all other life forms growing from the great body of the earth.

I think my mother really wanted to protect that place for us — the place of the unhurried mind. But the world caught up with me eventually, with all its fierce demands of doing and becoming. A vague sense of unease now haunts me whenever I'm not engaged in useful activity. Like most young people, I am now plagued by an obsession of "becoming someone" and "doing something with my life." I am no longer fully embedded in the experience of a life happening, but often feel outside of my life, looking at it, thinking about it. I often feel a sense of anxiety when I am questioned about my life. I feel compelled to come up with a tidy, comprehensible explanation for my existence, something I can offer in one quick, easy sentence. Images of overly concerned adult faces flood my imagination. They surround me in bunches and peer earnestly down at me asking: "So, just to be clear, what *are* you doing, exactly?"

I long to return to that innocent place of connection and simplicity that I knew in childhood. I yearn to be unbothered by this self-conscious awareness, turned outwards towards the judgments of others. I seek to turn my mind inwards, back to that original, self-existing flame.

Growing up I was aware that our free-flowing lifestyle seemed suspicious to other people. Our days didn't follow a reliable regimen of useful activity at all. In fact, our time was filled with the free-flow of imagination games, adventures in the woods, spontaneous art projects and musical outbursts, interspersed with storybook tea times and large gaps of gazing at clouds or marveling at the delicate designs traced by raindrops down the window. Reading and writing happened, and Mom did try to busy us with more serious activities like math every now and then, but overall there was a suspicious amount of spaciousness going on.

On weekday expeditions to the playground, the library or the grocery store, we were often met by furrowed brows and questions from grocery store clerks or other adults who, unlike us, were not allowed to move freely through the world before 3 p.m. "Why aren't you in school?" they would demand. "We homeschool!" we'd reply, defiantly. "Homeschool? What's that?!" they'd say, frowning. "How do you learn stuff? What's 2 + 2?" Or "How do you expect to be socialized?"

I often had the sense of being like an escaped convict, freed from a place I had no memory of, born into a world that promised my freedom but where everywhere loomed WANTED posters of three little girls with scraggly hair and homemade bows and arrows (and stuffed unicorns).

I had a subtle feeling of being an outsider. I was sometimes envious of my friends who went to school, because they seemed to have a simple, comforting sense of belonging to something. They fit in with what our culture valued as the good life, the right life, the "normal" life. My family and I were like pioneers, forging ahead into uncharted lands, exchanging the comfort of fitting in for Freedom and her inevitable companion, Loneliness. We were stepping out of the cultural bubble, a paradigm that wasn't serving us — but what was outside of it? Only us and a few other deserters, spread few and far between. We'd pass them sometimes, roaming the wastelands of industrial disappointment. We would wave encouragement, and call out, "Better shores ahead!" Although we did know many other unschooling families growing up, especially in Vancouver, there was no real community outside the schooling world, no "village." Looking back I know this was a loneliness for all of us.

For some of my school friends, I could see there was a certain comfort they got from being in school, and I experienced that comfort when I dropped into high school for grade ten and half of grade eleven. I felt a sense of relief to finally fit in with the mainstream and have a normal life. I no longer had to justify myself to people. I could explain my life in one quick easy sentence: "I go to high school." In school, my life was structured for me — there was a pre-existing system of meaning for me to slip into, and enough constant activity to keep me from questioning that meaning too deeply. For many of my friends, it wasn't until they graduated from high school that they encountered their first gap in the social busy-ness system. Suddenly, after a life of having most things scheduled for them, they were presented with the void, the great abyss of optional meaningfulness. Unless they chose to go to university right away, many of these friends experienced a period of deep questioning about themselves and their place in the world. For many of them, it was the first time they got a chance to even notice how they really felt about things. I, on the other hand, had been well acquainted with that unsettling, existential angst since childhood.

Our culture has a profound fear of space. We are pacified by activity, saved from having to fully face the radical and awesome reality of ourselves in an unfilled moment. When we have free time, we may encounter the bizarre and unnerving mystery of what we are and what's really going on here. We may suddenly realize the weirdness of the situation: we are these strange, highly self-conscious creatures, with all sorts of unpredictable thoughts and feelings, crawling around on a spinning rock in space. What?! We may begin to notice our bodies and all the feelings inside of them. We may begin to hear the faint murmuring of our hearts giving us feedback about our lives. We may begin to question things. We may be filled with strong desires and inspirations that lead us away from our current busy-filled circumstances.

What would happen if the whole western world took a month off of work? What if everyone alive had to sit and experience themselves and reality without distraction, even for just a week or two? Would we continue to live the way we currently do?

My sisters and I were forced to question the entire foundation of our culture's value system from the get-go. For us, life was always open-ended. We were allowed to plan and fill up our own time. This gave us a lot of freedom to check in with ourselves, our feelings, our inner voices, to find out what was really true for us. We were left to forge our own pathway through the wild wood. This was terrifying and empowering all at once. I think it meant that we got very used to the void, to space, from the beginning.

The greatest gift unschooling gave me was the space to discover myself. My challenge now, as an adult in an overly busy world, is to reconnect to that space. With the help of meditation and other body-centered practices, I am learning to fully experience my feelings and inspirations moment to moment, and to give myself permission to be as I am. These feelings and inspirations change over time. I will never be able to pin myself down or come up with a conclusion, once and for all, as to who or what I am. All I can do is be true to this ever-changing process of being a human being, and to share my current state with others.

When I look around at our world, I see that we are all trying to find our way back. Back to our hearts, back to the earth, back to a half-remembered joy we once inhabited in babyhood. Back to the present moment, back to our innocence, back to a sense of rightness and belonging. My hope for our world is that we can allow ourselves the time and space to fully *feel* our lives, our feelings, our bodies, and through our bodies feel our connection with all beings. I hope we can take a step back from the mind-made frenzy, and for a moment notice the trees, the wind, the stars. My wish is for all the children trying to navigate this strange world to be granted some free time. Because it is within the quiet empty space of non-doing that we discover who we are.

Chapter Fourteen
Siblings

Our siblings. They resemble us just enough to make all their differences confusing, and no matter what we choose to make of this, we are cast in relation to them our whole lives long.[32]

Susan Scarf Merrell

Having siblings is a mixed blessing. My three daughters are very close. They call each other often to share both good news and bad. They confide in one another when upset and love to celebrate special occasions together. But I have also noticed that they can be competitive.

During their childhood, birth order was definitely a determining factor. Marlise, when she was young, was always desperate to keep up with Lauren. If Lauren got a present for Christmas, Marlise would tend to think it was "better" than hers. If Lauren read a book, Marlise wanted to read the same one. Whatever Lauren was interested in, Marlise had to be interested in it too. Julia, the youngest of all, tried to copy everything her older sisters did when she was a toddler. She was fascinated by them and sought to model herself on their example. But being so much younger, she figured out early on that she couldn't keep up. Being the little tag-along wasn't a role Julia ever much relished.

Although the three girls have many interests and talents in common, I noticed that as they got older they began to specialize.

Lauren had always loved to draw and spent countless hours during her childhood creating art. Marlise also loved drawing and painting as a young child. (My mother-in-law, until she died, had a stunning landscape Marlise painted at age six hanging on her living room wall.) However, as the years passed Marlise gradually chose to yield this territory to Lauren and turned to music, an area in which Lauren didn't dominate. Julia, coming along behind her dynamic older sisters, got perhaps the worst deal. She is naturally both artistic and musical. But the turf in both these domains was already "taken" by her siblings.

I sometimes wonder whether there was any way I could have minimized this natural competitiveness between siblings so that Julia would have felt more free to explore her natural talents at an earlier age. I never compared the girls to one another and always welcomed and celebrated their creativity. Nonetheless, as she grew older, if Lauren and Marlise took up an activity, Julia tended to *not* want to do it. Rather than strain to keep up she preferred to opt out and go her own way.

It wasn't until Lauren left home to study Integrated Media in Vancouver that Julia's own art really began to take off. I can't tell if this was just due to her natural timetable, or whether having Lauren out of the house opened up some kind of emotional space for Julia. Perhaps the latency period of her early teens — when Julia spent a lot of time alone journaling and introspecting — was a necessary incubation period for the artist she would later become. Perhaps her timing has nothing to do with the presence or absence of her older sister. I will never know. I only know that Julia's keen passion for painting didn't develop until Lauren had moved away.

Verbal "airspace" was another issue among the girls as they grew up. Lauren, the oldest, was very articulate and communicative. She always had lots to say. Marlise, although an extrovert and very sociable and bubbly as a child, was more inchoate when she was with her older sister, because she was used to letting Lauren do the talking. Once Lauren left home, I noticed Marlise moving into the territory Lauren had vacated. Again, I will never be sure if this was a natural evolution of her personality, or whether family dynamics were a contributing factor. Marlise became the verbal and articulate one who loved to analyze social and philosophical issues, whereas Julia still tended not to contribute much to family conversations. As Marlise and Julia have spent more and more time apart during the past few years, this situation has changed again. Julia is becoming more forceful and decisive. She now shares her thoughts and opinions more freely with the rest of us. She says she still struggles with a younger sister's sense of not being listened to. But she is slowly learning to trust that she has as much to say as anyone else.

I don't believe birth order is the most determining factor by any means, but it shouldn't be underestimated. As parents we can't "save" our children from their position in the family system any more than we can save them from having us as their mother or father. Some things are just a matter of chance. Or fate. Or karma. To resist or resent the givens of life is pretty pointless. But siblings are a huge part of what shapes a child's personality, and I think it is important as parents to be sensitive to the dynamics between children. Perhaps a child who doesn't get much chance to talk when the whole family is together needs more opportunities for one-on-one conversations with Mom or Dad, for instance. Or two siblings who both love music or sports might be helped to find their own zone of competence, so that they aren't obliged to compete with one another.

In the end, how two siblings treat each other will depend most of all on how they are each treated by their parents. If we show our children respect and courtesy they will learn to treat each other kindly. If we show them unconditional love and approval, any natural rivalry between them won't become destructive. Competitiveness will be more than balanced by genuine appreciation for each other, and by faith that there is enough love to go around.

I notice more and more that my three adult daughters are each other's best supporters. They are very proud of each other's talents and abilities and love to be on hand to celebrate each other's triumphs. Perhaps the trick with sibling rivalry is to be patient when it occurs. If we can be relaxed and trusting that each child will blossom in her own time and in her own way, life will do the rest.

Chapter Fifteen
Sexuality and Other Awakenings

Love is the only sane and satisfactory answer to the problem of human existence.[33]

Erich Fromm

Having three daughters is bound to trigger some anxiety in any parent when it comes to their developing sexuality, and I was no exception. I longed for them to have healthy, loving "first" experiences; I wanted to protect them from abuse, or shame, or trauma. I hoped they would be able to enjoy long, leisurely childhoods, postponing the storm and stress of adolescence for as long as possible. Life, however, always has its own plans.

Both my older daughters suffered traumatic experiences in their teens that I wasn't able to protect them from. Lauren's first sexual experience was effectively a "date rape" at the age of sixteen. Marlise got pregnant when she'd barely turned sixteen and had an abortion. I thought at the time that I was being fully open with them about sexuality and birth control. But I see now that I was in denial to some extent: I didn't want to admit to myself how grown-up they were becoming. I wasn't ready for the precious, innocent years of middle childhood to be over. So I ignored the signs that the girls had become sexual beings.

When Lauren was almost sixteen she decided to go to high school on Salt Spring Island, commuting by water taxi fifty minutes each way. She worked hard at making new friends during the first semester, joined the choir and the school play, and by Christmas seemed to have been accepted by the other kids in grade eleven. What she didn't tell me, however, was that she felt embarrassed to still be a "virgin." Most of her new friends were already sexually experienced. Feeling pressured to fit in with the crowd, she went to parties with people she didn't really like or trust. At one of these gatherings, she was basically forced into having sex with an older teenaged boy. It was a wretched experience for her, and one she couldn't talk about for years. Our culture idealizes romantic love. Girls grow up watching Disney movies in which "love's first kiss" for the heroine occurs in the tender arms of Prince Charming. Instead, Lauren's first sexual encounter was ugly and unwanted. She felt ashamed.

How could I have protected her from such an experience? I don't think I could have. I wish that I had been more aware of the social pressures she was experiencing at school. I wish I had noticed that something was amiss. But I also have to realize that she chose not to share her feelings with me. She evidently needed to process this painful experience on her own.

Marlise had a much sweeter introduction to sexuality, but one that was also very challenging for us as her parents because she was still so young at the time. Marlise was the first to bring a boy home to meet us. Lauren had been attending high school for the past year, and when September rolled around Marlise decided she wanted to try high school on Salt Spring too. She was fifteen and enrolled in grade ten. Hardly two months went by before I learned she already had a boyfriend, a seventeen-year-old Salt Spring boy named Joshua (not his real name).

Here is my journal entry from January 2003:

Stressful weekend! Marlise brought Joshua home for a sleepover! I just don't know what to think about it all….

On Friday afternoon Marlise called home from school and asked if Joshua could come back to Mayne on the water taxi with her. I knew that since there is no evening ferry back to Saltspring, it would mean he would have to spend the night.

"Sure," I agreed cheerfully, and told her that Joshua could stay in the guest room in the basement.

Marlise wanted him to stay in her room with her. "He's kind of afraid of the dark," she said.

I think I just wasn't ready to put my mind around any of this. Marlise was such a kid only yesterday! How could it be possible that she wanted a boy to sleep in her room with her? I told her no. Joshua would have to sleep in the guest room and that he would be fine. He could leave the light on all night if he needed to.

Well, he arrived and we all liked him right away. He and Marlise seem to get along very well. They spent the evening after supper laughing and horsing around together like old buddies. When everyone seemed ready to call it a night, I showed our guest to his room and he appeared to go willingly. The lights went out and the house grew quiet. Then we heard a creak on the stairs.

"Richard!" I whispered, shaking him to wake him up. "Listen!"

"What?" said Richard, half-asleep.

"It's Joshua coming up the stairs! He's going up to Marlise's room!"

That woke him up. We both sat up in bed, feeling really tense, listening to the slow careful footsteps climbing up, up . . .

"What should we do?" I asked nervously. "You go talk to them!"

"Me?" said Richard. "I don't want to go talk to them! They'd be so embarrassed!"

"But she's only fifteen! She's too young!"

I think I half-expected Richard to leap to his feet and thunder angrily upstairs like a true father-defending-his-daughter's-virtue. Shotgun in hand, preferably!

He wouldn't budge.

"I'm tired," he finally said. "I'm going back to sleep."

Richard just rolled over and began to snore. Damn. I was left alone with my head spinning. I am ashamed to admit it, but what I kept wondering over and over was "What would the neighbours say?!" I particularly thought of M disapproving of my "permissiveness." The other day, talking about teenagers, she had proclaimed, "They need limits! They are looking to you to set the rules!"

Sigh. What are the rules in this case? Is there a "right" age for a teenager to begin to explore sexuality? How can a parent know if a young person is ready or not? I would feel a lot better about the situation if Marlise were eighteen, or even seventeen. But fifteen is so young!

I feel like our family has always been pretty open about sexuality. I talk about sex with the girls and they are comfortable asking questions. So why is this suddenly so hard? What am I really scared of?

I spent an hour that night lying in the dark exploring my feelings. First, as I said earlier, I was worried about others "finding out" that we had allowed our fifteen-year-old daughter and her boyfriend to sleep together under our roof. Would they think something was wrong with our family because our daughter was so precocious? Would we be seen as enabling an unhealthy situation? Second, I became aware of my own sadness at having my child grow up. Her new interest in Joshua was a clear sign that she was beginning to grow away from us, to form other attachments and a new identity in the world. I felt a sense of loss as well as fear.

After we dropped Joshua off at the ferry the next afternoon, Marlise and I had a talk. I explained to her that I knew Joshua had spent the night in her room and that at first I'd felt really uncomfortable about it but that I was trying to work through my discomfort. I wanted her to know that I trusted her to choose what was best for herself.

"Why is it such a big deal?" Marlise asked. "We just cuddled. We're not ready for sex yet."

"Oh," I hesitated, surprised. I'd apparently made a mountain out of a molehill.

"But you will be ready one day," I continued. "And when you are, I just want you to know, it's *fine* with me."

Marlise and Joshua did wait about six months before having sex. I realize now that I should have insisted that Marlise start taking the birth control pill even if they supposedly weren't "ready" yet. I just left it up to her to let me know if/when she needed help getting birth control. That was my mistake. She ended up getting pregnant and it was a traumatic experience for her to get an abortion.

I think Marlise experienced her own version of sexual shame. I think she felt guilty for not having prevented the pregnancy. But also she felt betrayed by her own body. She still thought of herself as a child. How could her body be ready to produce a baby?! The idea was deeply disturbing for her.

If I had those years to live again, there are things I would do differently. I would keep checking in, both with myself and with my children. I would try to stay aware of my own reluctance to let go of the idyll of childhood, so that it didn't cloud my vision and cause me to live in denial of what was really happening in my daughters' lives. Most young people today, in my experience, will begin to be interested in sex around age fifteen. Both Marlise and Julia had serious boyfriends at this age. Some teenagers will bloom earlier, some later, but for most the shift into adult sexuality seems to happen very suddenly, with little warning. Best to expect the transformation, realizing that it is gloriously human, powerful and inevitable, rather than practice wishful thinking that our children will stay innocent and attached to us until they leave home.

There are many pitfalls on the road of love. Parents cannot choose the course of their children's sexual awakening. We can't pick their partners for them, or decide when they are ready for a relationship. However, we can communicate to our children our deep faith that they will survive the inevitable trials and challenges of relationships. We can trust that they will continue to learn and grow stronger from each experience.

Both Marlise and Lauren learned a lot about themselves and about the world through their painful early experiences. Both have more compassion now for other girls and women who struggle, either with unwanted pregnancy or with humiliating sexual encounters, than they would have had without their own suffering. All three of my daughters have chosen kind, sensitive and thoughtful young men as partners. They are fully in charge of their sexuality and don't feel disempowered to be women.

Maybe the biggest lesson I have learned from watching the girls struggle with relationships and sexuality is simply — once again — to *trust life*. Keep your eyes and your heart wide open to what comes. As creatures we are deeply, fundamentally, resilient. We learn and grow all the time. When those around us witness and accept our experiences lovingly, we are free to move through those experiences no matter how painful or dark they may be.

Chapter Sixteen
Sharing the Journey

The greatest service we can offer anyone is to mirror their true heart.[34]

Stephen Levine

Who am I?

I was at a party a few years ago and fell into conversation with Marvin, a man who had just turned fifty. He was the principal of the small elementary school on our island at the time. He seemed happily married, with two grown sons. I didn't know him well, but he had always struck me as pleasant and friendly, if a little stiff. We joked about getting older, and about how hard it was to have our kids grow up and not need us much anymore, etc. Then, suddenly, his tone grew serious.

"Maybe it's just this stage of life," Marvin said shyly, "but I find myself asking for the first time . . . a lot of questions. I mean, I'm really happy and everything. I have all that someone could wish for. But I am having doubts. Do you ever find yourself wondering about things, asking certain questions like 'Who am I?' and 'What is it all for?'"

His face looked, for a moment, raw and vulnerable, as if he were confessing an embarrassing secret. I could tell he was afraid I would think him foolish. "I ask those questions all the time,"

I said, smiling at him reassuringly. "I've been asking them since I was a teenager. I guess I've just gotten used to not finding any answers." What I wanted to know, but didn't ask, was not why he was experiencing doubt about the meaning of life at his age. I wanted to know how he had managed to live so long — through half a lifetime — without wondering what it's all for.

I have always been highly introspective. The question "Who am I?" was a pretty constant companion from an early age. My mother tells me that once, when I was about six or seven years old, she heard me hollering out some urgent question from the bathroom where I was taking a bath. She hurried in to see what all the fuss was about. "What's wrong?" she asked. I was sitting naked in a froth of bubbles with a look of consternation on my face. "What's it all *for*?!" I repeated. "What's *what* for?" asked my mom. She figured I was questioning the necessity of bathing, perhaps, or why one had to use soap. "Life!" I replied. "What's *life* for?!"

By the age of twelve I began to have painfully intense episodes of self-consciousness that haunted me throughout my teenage years. These "spasms," as I called them, were sudden moments of acute dissociation — lasting only a few minutes   when I would feel as if I were waking from a dream to find that there was no outside to the dream, no "real" life to wake up to. It was a feeling of collapse, of contraction, of everything being horribly random and limited — like finding out that one was a character in a book one had been reading. The experience would leave me feeling drained and almost sick to my stomach.

When I attempted to describe this experience to others I found that no one understood what I was talking about. Was I going crazy? Why was I the only one suffering from this painful awareness?

I was so relieved when, finally, I met Richard (I was sixteen and he was seventeen) and learned he'd had a very similar feeling off and on for years. He told me the first time he'd been only eight years old. Walking home from school one afternoon, he'd come upon an earthworm slowly inching its way across the sidewalk.

He stopped and watched it for a while and was suddenly struck by the alien *thingness* of the worm. There was the worm, and there he was, also a *thing*, staring at it. He felt repelled. His eight-year-old mind realized that he too could have been born a worm. It was by the slimmest chance that he was a boy instead. Being alive seemed all at once random and unpredictable and absurd.

This experience of suddenly finding one's life random and alien and small is perhaps the most acute form of what my fifty-year-old friend Marvin was referring to as "questioning" life. The meaning and value of everything is cast into doubt. Psychologists call the extreme form of this feeling "depersonalization." They got the term from the French writer Henri-Frédéric Amiel, who first coined the word in his journal in 1880. He wrote, "I find myself regarding existence as though from beyond the tomb, from another world; all is strange to me; I am, as it were, outside my own body and individuality; I am depersonalized, detached, cut adrift. Is this madness?"[35]

As a young person, I experienced this feeling every month or two, but it never lasted very long. Some people, however, experience depersonalization continually, sometimes for years. Postings to the online sites dedicated to chronic sufferers of Depersonalization Disorder (DP, as they call it) are often heart-wrenching. People describe feeling "numb." "Nothing makes sense." Even once-familiar objects and people are drained of all meaning and value. Life becomes grey, tasteless and mechanical, without joy or vitality.

This severe form of dissociation from life is not to be wished on anyone. But I have learned to feel grateful for my early taste of detachment. The French philosophers call it *Le coup de vide*: the blow of the void. Yes, indeed, the blow hurts. When we first lift the veil of illusion — that comfortable screen of received ideas about meaning and purpose given to us by our culture — and glimpse the existential emptiness beyond, it can be terrifying. But it is also supremely freeing. I feel I owe my deep and stubborn independence of mind to this formative experience. Nobody can trick me by offering me pat answers to life's abiding questions, because I have seen where all answers fall short. The void is the ultimate bullshit detector: it never fails.

But I do believe that if I had never found anyone else, either in person or in print, to share and corroborate my feelings of depersonalization, they would have become more severe. Perhaps what we need most of all is the companionship of fellow questioners. Being alone with frightening thoughts is painful; being able to share them with others who are sympathetic makes them much easier to bear.

All three of my daughters have experienced episodes of dissociation from time to time as they were growing up. Here is an excerpt from my journal.

June 1995

I just had a long conversation with Lauren and Marlise about that "weird feeling" — that overwhelming consciousness of self it seems we are all prone to. It was uncanny hearing Lauren describe how it feels to her. She used almost the same words I remember writing in my journal as a teenager. Here is Lauren, age nine, describing it exactly.

"It's like I see myself moving around, doing things and suddenly I feel like I'm dreaming. And yet, I can't wake up. I'll never wake up. I hate thinking that that's all there is — this kind of dream — and then you die."

"I can even make myself have this feeling. All I have to do is concentrate. It makes me feel like I'm going to faint."

"I feel like I have four eyes. Two are here (pointing at her eyes) and two are back here somewhere, watching me (pointing behind her head)."

I told her I knew exactly what she was talking about — that I had often felt it, still do at times, and that the feeling of not being real never completely goes away. It's something you just live with. It's part of having an active, intelligent, imaginative mind. A painful part, but inescapable.

"Does it make you more comfortable to be able to talk about it?" I asked her. She nodded her head emphatically.

Marlise listened and joined in with her own point of view now and then. She too has told me that sometimes she "feels strange to be herself."

A dark feeling shared bravely with another never seems as dark and dangerous as one that remains unspoken and unshared. I was glad I could give my children the reassurance that no one gave me when I was first encountering the "weird feeling" of dissociation. It makes me wonder what would happen to those suffering from Depersonalization Disorder if someone would just affirm, for a moment, the truth of what they are experiencing. If someone could just say, "I know. I feel that too. It's part of being human and having this big human brain. Don't fight it. It's just life. We can be OK with it."

Even those who don't ever feel dissociated in the way I've described must inevitably confront the fact that they are dying creatures. Death knocks at everyone's door eventually, no matter how talented or wealthy or fit we are, no matter whether or not we have accomplished our goals. Death reminds us that nothing is permanent, not even ourselves.

Perhaps that is what Marvin meant when he referred to being at a "stage of life" when he couldn't help asking ultimate questions. Perhaps during his youth he never much doubted that all was right with the world. Perhaps he was so swept up in achieving goals set him by his family system, or his religion, or his culture, that he never awoke from the dream of identity, even for a moment. Now, however, at fifty, death is looming closer on the horizon. He can't hide any longer from the inevitability of his own demise. In the end, death makes us all question the "point" of our short time here in the world.

Stephen Jenkinson, grief counselor and speaker on the art of dying, says we live in a "death phobic" culture. The values of western civilization, he points out, stress competence, progress, rationality and self-mastery, rather than the living of a fully human life. We are educated to solve problems, to fix what's broken; we try to build institutions and structures that last. Death, however, puts the lie to all our dreams and aspirations, because it isn't a problem we can solve. No matter what drugs or treatments or procedures we subject the human body to, we all still die in the end. Unable to admit defeat, we opt instead to hide death out of sight in hospitals and funeral homes. We never talk about it. We try as much as possible to live as if we were never going to die.

This is a mistake. Jenkinson speaks passionately about our need to bring death back to its rightful place at the heart of our communities. Yes, awareness of death hurts. It is "the wound of your life," "the recognition that your love and respect and praise will not save anyone or anything from suffering, from infirmity or from dying away." But death is also the "angel" that teaches us to cherish life. In Jenkinson's words, "our ability to be grateful doesn't come from worthy things lasting forever. It comes from knowing that they will not last, and from loving that too," from "remembering with grace . . . the ragged, uncertain immensity of life, of which our lives are a small and magnificent part."[36]

Sensitive children wake early to the knowledge of mortality. The death of a grandparent or a friend or a beloved pet has a profound impact on a child. They begin asking questions like "Why are we here?" as soon as they realize that they, too, will one day die. In a culture that fears death, however, most parents are uncomfortable with such questions. Many of us have an aversion to grief. We don't know how to share our children's sorrow simply and openly. Instead, we feel obliged to "focus on the positive," saying things like "Grandma had a good life, so it's OK," or "her suffering is all over now." Too scared to open our hearts to the immense sorrow of loss, we hide behind platitudes.

But when we don't allow ourselves to grieve, we shut down our capacity to feel alive. We stay on the surface of our experience, unable to cherish what we have because we won't acknowledge that we will lose it. We miss out on deep connections with one another and with the world around us. As the poet Wallace

Stevens said, "Death is the mother of beauty."[37] Death is also the mother of love. Death teaches us to fall in love with life, to feel deeply grateful for our brief, bright time here in the world. Grief and gratitude are two sides of the same coin; we value what is, because we know it will soon be gone.

Our willingness to grieve, to acknowledge the dying away of everything, is a great gift to our children. If we are not frightened by the mystery and sorrow of being alive, our children won't be either. They take their cue from us. It doesn't matter what, in the end, we say in response to their questions, or their fears, or their sadness. To be reassuring, we don't have to have answers. We just have to be brave and honest, to admit that life hurts at times. We have to stay close, to hug them as we talk, and let them know that human intimacy is a match for even the darkest thoughts. Sharing the grief of life deepens the bonds between us. I felt, for instance, closer to Marvin as he shared his vulnerable uncertainty than at any previous time we had met. Grief and love spring from the same well.

Chapter Seventeen
Holding Until Relaxed

Befriending our experience — by making space for what is, along with all our feelings about it — is what facilitates movement.[38]

John Welwood

One of the hardest challenges we face is to witness another's suffering. There are times when the sight of another's pain calls us to action: we rush to pull a car accident victim from a burning vehicle, for instance, or leap into a frigid river to rescue a child from drowning. But sometimes there is nothing we can do. At such times we help not by acting but by staying still and open, by bearing witness — without judgment — to the life that is unfolding, here and now.

The other day I was walking along the beach with a distraught friend who had just confessed that she thought she should divorce her husband. I was shocked. I'd always observed that she and her husband were very close. They had been together for twenty-five years and had raised a child whom they were both very fond of. They seemed genuinely to appreciate and enjoy each other's company. My first thought was that she was making a big mistake.

Despite appearances, the relationship was evidently in trouble, though. Years of unvoiced hurt and resentment had brought things to a breaking point. My friend, nearly hysterical, felt the marriage "just couldn't work anymore." She was frantically making plans for how they could separate and live apart, despite the fact they had very little money. She said she couldn't sleep at night because she felt so deeply sad.

I wanted to argue with her, to persuade her to reconsider. Her plans for the future sounded desperate and impractical. Her appraisal of the present situation also seemed distorted; I was worried she was going to ruin her life because of some negative thoughts that had taken hold of her mind. I was also scared that she would affect my life for the worse, since Richard and I really enjoyed socializing with her and her husband as a couple. If they split, we would all lose out.

But the last thing my friend needed in that moment was for me to try to talk her out of her feelings. What she needed most was to have her pain and sadness and disappointment witnessed. My job as her friend was to stand calm and unafraid at her side as the dark storm of feeling passed through her. My gift was to keep on loving her no matter what she chose to do with her life.

The "first noble truth" about existence, as the Buddha said, is that *Life is suffering*. Each day brings its particular challenges and hardships. Each phase of life is beset with struggle and disappointment and, occasionally, heartache. Not that life is without moments of transcendent joy and beauty. But suffering accompanies us, like the shadow we cast on a sunny day, wherever we go. To be alive is to know change and loss and impermanence. Life hurts as often as not.

The thing about suffering is that the more we resist it, the more it hurts. And I have noticed that if we anxiously antici-pate pain, before anything has even yet gone wrong, we are more likely to invite disaster. The very dread of suffering begets more suffering.

Parents should take this to heart. We are all prone to worry. Life is dangerous. All manner of evils could befall our children, from physical injury to emotional trauma. We cannot protect our children from life. But if we continually express anxiety about their well-being we will make things a lot worse. Our children will learn to be cautious, self-doubting and fearful of the future. If we communicate our deep faith in human resilience, on the other hand, they learn that they can cope with whatever life throws at them.

Here is another way of stating this paradox: *When you worry about your children, you draw down curses on them. When you trust your children you draw down blessings.*

The "curse" of worry is perhaps most noticeable when it comes to physical courage. I have observed, for example, that anxious parents often have disaster-prone children. When my daughters were young we all loved to go to the playground in our local park. Sometimes we'd encounter a child who seemed nervous and tentative on the play equipment. This child would usually turn out to have a parent who hovered over her as she played, offering advice and warnings: "Don't climb too high, you might fall!" "Careful on that swing!" "Don't run so fast, you'll trip!" This careful child was the one who tended to fall and get hurt. The parent's lack of trust in the child's instincts caused the child to mistrust herself. All that worry seemed to draw down the "curse" of more falls, more scrapes, more injuries.

Anxiety over physical danger is perhaps easier to spot than anxiety over emotional well-being. So many of us fall into worrying about whether or not our children are "happy" or "well-adjusted" or "popular" or "talented" without realizing that, just like the nervous mother on the playground, we are drawing down curses on our children's tender, struggling spirits. Our worrying, in fact, confirms their secret fears that they are not, indeed, OK. Disaster must loom on the horizon or Mom wouldn't be in such a tizzy.

I used to worry a lot more about my children than I do now. I might still be a worrier if it weren't for Julia. I had an experience with her many years ago that changed me forever; it made me see clearly that worry is damaging to relationships. Unconditional acceptance and respect, on the other hand, are powerfully healing.

Julia went through a very uncomfortable period in her early teens. Even as a young child, she had always been extremely sensitive and thoughtful. The existential crisis that hit my friend Marvin at age fifty hit Julia very young. When she was eleven she began to seem to me unusually insecure and self-conscious. I felt anxious about her. Was she lonely? Bored? At that time, she didn't have any clear passions or hobbies and resisted my attempts to sign her up for classes or to introduce her to new children. I fretted about what I thought was her lack of self-esteem. Was it her position in the family — the fact that she was youngest, with two very dynamic and creative older sisters? Or was the problem the fact that we lived in a rural setting with few other kids her age around? I couldn't bear to see her unhappy.

I began taking Julia into town for a couple of days each week so that she could meet other homelearning kids her age. She enjoyed the trips to town, and even made some friends, but nothing seemed to really make her happy.

Richard and I would lie awake at night and wonder "what's wrong with Julia?" Richard worried that she was isolated and bored and thought she might be happier at school. I felt sure that if only she could find her "thing" — that special passion that would make her feel engaged and successful — everything would magically improve for her. The result of our parental conferences was that whenever Julia appeared frustrated or depressed, Richard would urge her to try going to school. I would counter by suggesting all the different kinds of classes, workshops and mentorships she might try. All to no avail. Julia just kept saying no, and seemed even more discouraged by our efforts to help.

Then one day it all changed. Here is my journal entry for that day. Julia was fourteen.

September 2005

Today marked a big turning point in my relationship with Julia. I feel a huge sense of relief, as if something dark and heavy that has been weighing me down for months just melted away.

This morning Julia was in a particularly dark mood. She hardly talked to me at breakfast. Afterwards, she spent a long time staring gloomily out the living room window. Of course, seeing her sitting there looking miserable pushed all my buttons immediately, all my anxiety triggers: She's not happy! Something's wrong with her life! I am a lousy mother!

I went into the living room all cheery and sat down next to her. I began to suggest all the things she might like to do that day. "You know," I said brightly, "we are all happier when we have projects on the go, things we can pour our energy into and get a feeling of accomplishment from." Each of my suggestions met with sullen refusal. Her face got darker and more wretched as she listened. Finally she burst into tears and said, "You and Dad are always worrying about me, always trying to fix me. Don't you know that when you do that it makes me scared?"

She stomped upstairs and spent the rest of the morning barricaded in her room. I was stunned. I'd never considered that we were making her afraid of herself, of her own reality. Wow. I had to think about that . . .

Later, in the afternoon, the sun came out and I saw through the kitchen window that Julia had gone outside and was lying on the trampoline staring up at the sky. I went outside, kicked off my shoes and climbed up with her. We lay like that in silence for a long time, watching the clouds drift slowly across the vast blue emptiness. I let myself completely relax. I opened my heart to whoever and wherever Julia was, right then, right there.

Slowly, she began to talk. She talked about how meaningless life seemed, how uncomfortably weird the universe was. Yes, I answered. I, too, knew these dark feelings intimately. The universe is so weird. And it's so hard, sometimes, to be alive — so difficult to carry these eyes around in our heads, this painful consciousness of all the loss, all the disappointment, all the change, all the dying around us. "And it seems like no one ever really understands anyone else," said Julia. "We're all so alone."

It was such a beautiful moment. We lay there trading quiet comments about fear, about longing, about loneliness. Side by side, gazing up at the great weird universe, we shared the pain of the human condition. I was no longer the mother, the caregiver, and she the child. We were two fellow travellers on this strange journey of existence. I don't know how long we spent on the trampoline that day, but at some point Julia turned towards me smiling. Her face was light and relaxed in a way I hadn't seen for months. "I love you, Mom!" she said.

The dark, heavy layer that dissolved during that afternoon on the trampoline was my own anxiety. I chose to stop worrying. The change in me didn't magically transform Julia into a cheerful, contented adolescent. But it took away any sense that there was a *problem* to be solved. Julia relaxed. She felt welcome, finally, to be exactly who she was, here and now.

Over the past seven years I have watched Julia blossom into a thoughtful, empathetic and self-reliant human being who is drawn to philosophical and spiritual investigations. She will always be highly sensitive and prone, at times, to dark moods. But she no longer feels stuck. And she has also "found her thing" — at least her thing for now. She has become a passionate artist whose paintings hang all over our house. What I anxiously thought of as her "depression" was just the natural expression of where she was at that stage of her life-path.

A year or two after our moment on the trampoline Julia said to me, "I realize now that when I start feeling hopeless and depressed, it's just a mood and will pass. I used to think I had to take these moods seriously — that they were the *truth* and that everything else was illusion. Now I realize they are just like clouds passing in the sky. They come and they go again."

What I most value now is that Julia shares her feelings and thoughts with me readily, trusting that I will listen without trying to offer advice. Four years ago the two of us walked for a whole month (500 miles) along an ancient pilgrimage route in southern France. We walked side by side for six or seven hours a day, talking about everything under the sun, as easy and companionable as old, old friends.

Young children, like adolescents, have ups and downs. They learn early on that life is often painful. They fall ill or get injured. They are teased or shunned on the playground. Family members or pets die, toys are lost or broken, friends move away. There is simply no way to design family life so that our children never experience disappointment, frustration or sadness. Dark feelings come with the territory. They are part of what makes us human.

Our gift, as parents, is to help our kids feel OK with what is happening, since they often don't know how to do this for themselves. Whenever my young daughters would get over-tired, or over-stimulated, or were frustrated or disappointed in some way, they often couldn't soothe themselves. They would start to fidget, or whine or cry. Sometimes they would even lash out physically, at me or at each other. If I was too busy to stop and help them deal with their experience, things would only go from bad to worse; if I scolded them, or gave them a "time out," or in any other way withheld my love and approval, their misery would usually escalate into a full-blown tantrum. Whatever initial problem had upset them was now eclipsed by their sense of rejection by me.

If, during these difficult moments, I was able to give love instead of withhold it, everything changed almost instantly. If, instead of punishing, I gathered my angry, upset child into my arms and held her for a while, her negative feelings would immediately begin to subside. Safe in the circle of my arms, my child's anger and whining would turn to sobs. Grief flowed as we held each other. Sometimes I would ask her what was wrong, but more often I didn't need to. Just *allowing* her to experience her powerful negative feelings was cure enough. A short time later I would feel all the tension drain from her small body. She would relax in my arms and her sobs would slow and then cease altogether. Before I knew it she would be off and playing again, all trace of the tantrum gone. I would be free to go back to whatever task I had been working at.

In my experience, there is a law of cause and effect that governs our emotional nature: *Whatever you resist persists.* Punishing a child for her feelings is a guarantee that those feelings will become even more overwhelming for the child and more disruptive for everyone else. Fights can go on for hours and dominate the whole house, leaving everyone in the family exhausted. On the other hand, expressing love when someone is angry with you — though admittedly often hard to do — works like magic. It's amazing how a simple hug can restore harmony in a mere few minutes.

Being present with others is like holding them in an intangible embrace. Our unjudging attention makes them feel safe and seen and loved. Feeling unconditionally loved leads to relaxation — and relaxation, I believe, is the key to everything. The wisdom taught in every form of bodywork is that our muscles tend to hold on to tension. Bringing awareness to various parts of our body, through meditation or yoga, allows those areas to relax. *Tension dissolves with awareness.* When we hold each other — either physically, or emotionally through compassionate listening — we allow space for awareness. We help each other bring attention to the knots and tangles of emotional tension within us, which begins to loosen their hold. As a nurse once explained to me, "the body only heals when relaxed." Same goes for the heart. Relaxation allows for resilience and healing. It makes us loose and adaptable, both physically and emotionally.

Both the hysterical toddler and the moody adolescent want more than anything to be emotionally held by their parents. They want to feel safely, undeniably and deeply accepted, no matter what their experience, so that they can release the tension in their bodies and hearts and move on. Our primary job as parents is to create this zone of safety, this space of relaxation, for our children. I believe it is the best gift we humans can give, not only to our children but to one another. Only within the safe space of unconditional, loving acceptance can any of us acknowledge and release the many griefs of existence. When we feel loved we are able to move from mad or "bad" to sad, and then from sad to free. Our hearts stay open to the beauty of the world.

Art as Magic

By Julia Iredale

Insert 4

Growing up in my house was a constant whirlwind of activity. As kids, I and my sisters and our friends never settled for being one person, living one life. We were constantly imagining worlds, putting on characters, acting out alternate realities. In the space of one day we could be pirates, faeries, runaway orphans, wolves, selkies and unicorns. There was never an end to what we could imagine, or what we would endeavour to create.

I think that the greatest thing that my parents did for me as a child was just to let me explore and to play with various ways of bringing my imagination to life. I was able to develop a private world of my own, and to see how I could make my life beautiful and meaningful for myself in my own way. When I first started painting, in my early teens, nobody tried to teach me what to do, or asked me to explain my paintings. No one tried to categorize my style. I think this was really important. Creating art was a private process that I was free to explore without anyone leaning over my shoulder. I learned to value my own interpretation, my own insights and my own ideas, and to see that those were the greatest companions that I would be taking with me on the road of life. Nobody else was going to come along and tell me how to think, what to value or how to feel. I learned that my own instincts were all I had to go by, and that the world I lived in was a mysterious and changeable place, shaped by my own perceptions.

This urge to create has never really gone away. I feel very similar to my sisters in this way. We all share an extremely intense fascination with life's possibilities — with what can happen when you create an experience, an image or a song, or when your sense of life changes, for a second, and you find yourself on the border of a strange new country called the world.

Writer and activist Starhawk describes magic as "the ability to change consciousness at will." With this definition, I would describe art as magic. I believe that we, as humans, have a vast ability to experience life from many different angles. Art is not an exclusive party; all creative intelligence is invited. Every human being, if left to search out the wellspring of their inspiration, will find that they are a conduit for the ceaseless, creative forming of the universe.

Creative work is not always seen as "practical" or valuable by society at large. You cannot easily quantify its value — just as you cannot easily quantify the value of a life experience. Most of the things that people really value, such as love, freedom, a sense of meaning, are intangible and impossible to weigh. As I have grown older, I have witnessed how in our society we have set up systems that attempt to reduce the magic of life to a series of dollar signs, placards and certificates of achievement.

I just finished third year at Emily Carr University, where I have been majoring in Illustration. Attending an "art institution" has been an interesting experience. Let me start by saying that I have learned an incredible amount from my time at the school. It is hard to imagine that I would've worked as hard on my art were I not attending classes and meeting constant deadlines. All the gifts of school aside, it has been fascinating to approach school as an unschooler. I am definitely not impervious to the atmosphere that school creates. Like my classmates, I seek my teacher's good opinion and am affected by the atmosphere of competition created by the grading system and the constant peer critiquing. At the same time, in the back of my mind, I notice how the whole system drains my actual drive to create art.

My program is career focused, and there is a lot of talk about job markets, networking and what to expect in the illustration industry. While all of this is no doubt helpful, the focus seems to be on creating ourselves as desirable products that the world will want to buy. The whole world is then viewed as a game — play your cards right, appeal to different markets, get paid big money to do what you do, and boom, you've won. There is very little discussion about why we create art, what our motives are, what we want people to experience through our art, etc. Art has become another commodity in our commodity-based culture. We are now able to quantify the value of art by measuring its monetary value, the hype surrounding it and the size of its audience. We don't seem very interested in the experience of the artist, or in the power of the offering. We don't explore where the inspiration for art comes from in the first place.

People consume images in this culture like they consume everything else. I remember one day in class watching my friend scanning an art blog on her computer. Her finger kept scrolling and scrolling. Her eyes would alight on one magnificent, detailed image after the next. Now and then she would stop for a moment to click "like" before she scrolled down to the next piece. A work of art that took weeks or perhaps months to create flipped through her awareness in about two seconds.

Perhaps this "art as commodity" phenomenon is just another result of our spiritually starved and numbed-out culture. Art, instead of deepening and enriching our lives, has become like everything else — another thing for the passive observer to sit back and consume. Art school is not an oasis for the seers and the feelers of our society to seek each other out and transform their culture from within. Instead it has become the place where we go to lay down our gifts on the altar of the last god standing in our spiritually broken world: the dollar sign.

I believe that as creative people we have to watch out that the experience and the inspiration behind our work is authentic. We have to begin by living what we create. Within the school system, the emphasis is on output. Everything is subject to a weighing process. Within that system, how can we help but turn our eyes outward looking for someone else to tell us what is of value? It is a dangerous situation for art, because when we lose this reverence for our own personal experience art becomes lifeless, like a fire without fuel.

The artists I know who seem the most stoked on life don't worry much about how others see them. Many of them never even went to art school. They are coming from a place of fullness, of joy and optimism, rather than a place of lack. They love making art because they think it's awesome. They love sharing it. It's amazing to be around them. They don't try to be the "best" or the "most successful." Yet I think they are the ones that actually get out there and create; they are productive, and get invited to do all sorts of things. In the end, everyone actually wants to be around energy like theirs — energy that is beautiful and positive and open and loving.

It has been an amazing privilege to grow up in my family, among like-minded spiritual seekers who have always placed so much value on life's creative processes and challenges. As an art maker and as a life liver, my highest goal is to feel deeply and to experience the world intensely. I want to taste the beauty and the loss, the pain and the laughter of life. I want to keep filling my cup to the brim with the poetry of living.

Chapter Eighteen
Conscious Leadership

One does not become enlightened by imagining figures of light but by making the darkness conscious.[39]

Carl Jung

Young children don't always know what they need. They come into the world with no concept of "self." They begin life unaware of having a temperament and a body with needs and drives. Only gradually do they begin to build a coherent picture of themselves as separate and unique people. When children are young and still not self-aware, the loving adults in their lives need to be mindful for them. We show genuine leadership as parents when we are able to stay aware of what is arising in each moment for our children. When we see what is really going on for them, we are much better able to help them thrive.

I have found that being a good and sensitive *leader* sometimes means saying no to a child's request. Here is an example from my journal. Marlise's friend Michelle had been for a sleepover. The two nine-year-olds had been in each other's constant company for over thirty hours.

October 1997

Marlise is furious at me. Michelle slept over last night and now the two want to go back to Michelle's house for another sleepover. But I said no. The two girls had a great time all day yesterday and today — they put on "funny shows" for hours, they wrote songs and baked cookies and walked to the park. Last night I heard them whispering and giggling until the wee hours. They didn't want the party to end. But I could see that they were both exhausted!

Marlise got nearly hysterical when I said that they both now needed some alone time and that Michelle's mom was coming to pick her up. She was like a junkie panicking at the prospect of withdrawal. "It's going to be so boring!" wailed Marlise. "I'll have nothing to do. Why can't I go to Michelle's?" On and on it went.

Elaine (Michelle's mom) picked Michelle up just before dinner. Once they were gone, Marlise collapsed in angry tears on the carpet. "I'm bored!" she said to me angrily. I usually never hear those words except when she is feeling really stressed and over-stimulated. I sympathized with her, reassured her that she would see Michelle again soon, then got busy getting dinner ready. After a while Marlise's grumbling stopped. I looked over and saw that she had fallen asleep! She slept right through dinner, woke up for an hour or two, and then went back to bed. Next day she was back to her old self again, relaxed and pleasant to be with.

Marlise couldn't say no to the chance to keep playing with Michelle. She didn't realize that she was exhausted, but I, who knew her so intimately, could see it very plainly. She thought she wanted more stimulation, but I knew that she was actually stressed and unhappy and needed relief. My intervention, though unwelcome at first, ultimately made her feel safe.

Children who are tired don't always know they need to rest. When they are restless they can't always find ways to burn off steam. When a child feels trapped by her experience, when the pressure of unmet needs gets too strong, a "tantrum" usually results. Tantrums are a cry for help. They are a signal that a child doesn't know a way out of her distress.

Writer and parenting adviser Naomi Aldort says that parents need to provide what she calls "leadership" for their children. But by "leadership" she doesn't mean top-down, power-over decision making. She does not mean coercion or intimidation or force of any kind. Instead, she writes, parents provide leadership . . .

> . . . *by noticing what the child needs and creating the conditions for meeting that need in a safe way. She may need a space to run and scream; she may need the outdoors in order to climb, get muddy and throw stones in the water; she may need to experience independence and autonomy by making a mess of her toys or clothes. She also needs us to stop her from taking unsafe or unsuitable actions. She relies heavily on this kind of leadership because without it she cannot dare to spread her wings further and further.*
>
> *When leadership is insufficient, the child feels he has no one to rely on and trust. The results of lack of appropriate leadership and lack of trust and respect add up over time and result in stress, self-doubt and a sense of insecurity. The child feels lost and is likely to keep doing things that he hopes may force his parents into leadership — things that parents often perceive as "misbehaving" or as being overly demanding.* [40]

A leader is someone who has greater consciousness of all that is at work in the present moment than those she is leading. A leader is a careful and unjudging observer. She "sees" what those depending on her need, even when they can't see it for themselves. If a child is tired and fretful, a parent shows leadership by arranging for that child to rest. If she is frightened or upset, a parent provides comfort and reassurance. If she is full of frustrated energy, her parent helps her find an outlet such as a run in the park or a chance to dance to music.

Children rely on our greater level of awareness to feel safe. Sometimes we aren't able to meet a child's actual need in the moment because it conflicts with the needs of others. If we acknowledge her frustration and disappointment at such times we can maintain her trust. As Aldort explains, "If an activity has to be interrupted, the child's trust in our leadership will help her to accept the rarely imposed limit. When we have to leave the playground, we can take our child home as gently as possible and validate her crying with words, listening and hugs." When our children trust that we will always try our best to respect and accommodate their needs they more readily accept the occasional times when those needs just can't be met. They also feel safer knowing that the needs of everyone in the family are being acknowledged. Children, just like adults, feel most comfortable when there is harmony in the relationships around them. They won't thrive if their needs are being met time and time again at the expense of others.

Parents show leadership by creating safe, nurturing environments for their children to grow in. Keeping the kitchen shelves stocked with nutritious food instead of junk food, for instance, allows children to choose for themselves what they want to eat — but only from a range of healthy alternatives. Making sure the weekly schedule doesn't get too busy ensures that children have the space they need to absorb everything they are learning.

One of the greatest responsibilities of parenting is to choose consciously what to allow into our homes and lives, for everything in a child's environment becomes a shaping influence. Although we had a DVD player for watching occasional movies, Richard and I decided not to have television, as another way to keep "junk" out of the environment. We both felt that so much of what is shown on TV, particularly in the advertisements, promotes a consumerist, materialistic world view quite toxic for the young human soul. We also didn't want our kids to sit mesmerized in front of a screen for hours every day. Instead, we provided a house full of books, art supplies, tools, musical instruments, and toys that encouraged imaginative play. We also spent many hours with our children hiking, canoeing, biking and exploring the outdoors, because we wanted them to feel at home in the natural world.

Children need help pursuing their passions for learning as well. A parent provides loving leadership for her child first by noting what fascinates him. She observes the light that shines in his eyes when he is curious and engaged, and helps him explore what most entices him, be it a new Lego set, a beach covered in shells and driftwood, or the wonderful creatures in the Bug Museum. She may help him find mentors or classes that further his interests. She also recognizes when the child has had enough. Most interests change with time. When a child wearies of any particular activity or pursuit, a loving parent helps him leave it behind without shame.

Being a good leader is an extremely subtle art. All too often one's own unconscious fears or desires get in the way of true observation. When her child expresses negative emotions in public, for instance, a parent who is not acting consciously will succumb to worry that others will disapprove of her parenting. She won't *see* the child, because she is flooded with her own anxiety about "not being good enough" in the eyes of others.

Here is an excerpt from my journal written in 1992. Julia was a year old. An old friend from college whom I hadn't seen in years had arrived to visit, along with his new girlfriend.

What a horrible evening! Dave showed up at 4:00 with Liz, his new girlfriend (who just finished a degree in primary education) and even though I was feeling pretty exhausted, I felt obliged to invite them to stay for dinner. Julia was having a late afternoon nap, and the older girls were playing with their Playmobile, so I managed to have almost a full hour of conversation uninterrupted. But just around the time I was starting to wonder what the heck I was going to cook for supper, the baby woke up and wailed. Almost on cue, Marlise started to squeal because Lauren apparently "stole" her Playmobile pony. Lauren then began to act incredibly bratty — it was weird. Like she was deliberately trying to show the visitors just how obnoxious a six-year-old can be! At one point she even pulled down her pants and mooned my guests! I blew up at Lauren and sent her to her room, but of course she didn't stay there. I was so embarrassed. I kept wondering what Liz thought of me. She seemed full of sage advice about parenting, now that she was a certified teacher (even though she had no kids of her own yet). I am sure she thought I was completely incompetent, and that my kids were orangutans! Thank god Richard came home and helped. It was a pretty miserable evening. The girls bickered and fidgeted and cried all through dinner. Eventually David and Liz excused themselves and beat a hasty retreat. Sigh . . .

After my guests went home and Julia was back in bed, I had time to give Lauren and Marlise some attention. They calmed down once I wasn't so entirely preoccupied with playing host to my visitors. I realized that what they had needed all along was just a little reassurance from me that they were still loved. I had been ignoring them — so caught up as I was in trying to impress my guests. Feeling ignored, the children naturally began to experience stress and anxiety. They did whatever they could to get some attention from me. When that attention was negative (when I got angry and punished Lauren by banishing her to her room, for instance), it just made matters worse. The anxiety flooding their little bodies increased even further, resulting in even more disruptive behaviour.

That day back in 1992, I wasn't showing good leadership. I was not aware of what I myself was feeling and needing, and therefore wasn't able to understand the feelings and needs of the others in the room with me. I longed to connect with my visitors. I wanted them to think well of me. I was afraid of their judgment. My friends, on the other hand, had desires of their own. They were here on a visit from New York. They wanted to make their trip interesting by having a lively conversation. My children, in turn, needed to feel included in the interaction. They wanted reassurance that I hadn't forgotten or overlooked them.

In the end, no one's needs were met. We all ended up feeling frustrated.

Finding a way for everyone to get their needs met is only possible when we are *present* — that is, aware of what is actually going on, here and now. When children become disruptive, for instance, it's time to stop and reflect. It is time to "see" them, without judgment or resentment. It is also time to become aware of how we ourselves are being emotionally triggered by the situation. When we press the pause button and really attend to what is happening, solutions begin to appear.

If I had been mindful during that unfortunate visit, things might have turned out very differently. I might have shown leadership by choosing to include the children in our conversation for a while so that they felt more engaged. Or I might have said to Dave and Liz, "I really want to continue our conversation. I think the kids need to burn off some steam. Shall we take a walk to the park, so we can keep talking while they play on the swings?" I might also have simply excused myself for a few minutes.

Realizing that the children just needed a few minutes of my undivided attention, I could have asked my friends to wait while I read the girls a story, or while I found some paper and crayons so they could draw at the table next to us. I could also have been honest about my *own* needs. I could have admitted that I was too exhausted to cook dinner for them; how about ordering pizza?

Whenever we are able to stay relaxed and non-judging, we help everyone in the room feel safe. Their needs have been seen and acknowledged. No one feels blamed. And I have often noticed that once we express empathy, all people — even young children — become much more ready to accommodate the needs of others. Empathy leads to relaxation, and relaxation leads to resilience. A little attention really does go a long way.

Of course, we are only human. We all, occasionally, lose our tempers. But, with practise and patience, we can become more skillful leaders. We can learn to listen better. We can more ably perceive our children's needs and find ways for those needs to be met. The more we practice compassion, the stronger our capacity for it will grow.

Our children need the gift of compassionate leadership from us. But our role, I believe, changes with time. When children are young and still very unaware of themselves, they need us to help them know how they are feeling. As children mature, they become more able to recognize and articulate their own needs. Gradually, a parent's role changes. Eventually, we no longer provide leadership so much as empathy and support. I have found with my teenaged and adult children that the best gift I can offer now is simply to listen.

My three daughters are now very self-reliant. They plan and make choices knowing they are responsible for their own lives. They still, however, occasionally seek me out when they feel confused and uncertain. Whether they are wondering whether to quit college, or how to handle a difficulty in a relationship, or whether to move to a new town, they want a sympathetic ear. After twenty-seven years of apprenticeship in this wonderful and challenging art of parenting, I have learned not to give advice. Expressing doubt about my children's choices, or trying to control their decisions, produces no good outcome for them or for me. If, driven by my own anxiety, I interfere in their lives, I will cast a pall on our relationship that might take years to lift.

My job now, as it has been all along, is to love them unconditionally. Whenever I start to get anxious about something they are doing or saying, I try to remind myself that my daughters are writing *their* stories, not mine. Whatever choices they make will lead to further possibilities and choices. All paths lead to growth and learning. I don't attempt to foresee where the tale is heading. That would be unhelpful and unloving. What I can do is to explore, alongside them, what they are feeling and thinking right here and right now. I can be a sounding board so that they are able, in conversation with me, to clarify what is stirring in their hearts.

What keeps us from being good leaders for our children is what Marshall Rosenberg says hinders all loving communication between people: our "unresolved grief."[41] Most of us carry unhealed wounds within us — the traces of accumulated pain from a lifetime of not feeling fully accepted and loved by others. Most of us have been injured by judgment or rejection or blame; in fact, no one who grows up in a coercive, punitive culture such as ours is free of such wounds to the heart. Like tightly closed fists, these wounds cling to their tension far below the level of consciousness, often for decades. We don't trust others to be wholly and completely "on our side." Yet, if never shared, never consciously grieved, these painful emotions become blocks to our heart path. They prevent us from feeling the body's natural vitality and joy.

Whenever I judge or resist the words or actions of one of my children, it is always due to my own unconscious baggage: some old fear in me is triggered by their behaviour, some anxiety about not being "good enough" or "popular enough" or "safe enough." When I stop, breathe, observe what is really going on and ask myself "where is the problem?" usually there turns out to be no problem at all.

Unconscious pain causes us to be dangerous to others. "Hurt people hurt people," as the saying goes. Our babysitter Jackie was quick to condemn five-year-old Lauren because, most likely, she herself had been so thoroughly blamed and punished as a child. Her own "unresolved grief" at not being unconditionally loved and heard resulted in an inability to hear and offer love to another. As Rosenberg points out, unresolved grief blocks empathy. People in pain are more likely to attempt to control others in order to minimize further hurt. When we are flooded with anxiety — which is the body's response to the anticipation of further pain — we don't show up in the present moment. By not listening with an open and non-judgmental heart, we "draw down curses" on each other. We try to forestall further disaster by insisting that those around us behave in ways we believe will make us feel safer. We become bossy or manipulative or accusing or whiney. We communicate violently rather than lovingly.

The beautiful thing about the journey of parenting is that we are given chances every day to wake up and know ourselves better. Being with our children teaches us a whole lot about who we are. When our anxiety or anger is triggered we can learn to stop and ask ourselves, "What is going on right now inside me? Where do these powerful feelings come from? Why am I so resistant to who my child is at this moment?" Memories of our own childhood experiences may suddenly grip us. We may recall being criticized or blamed or rejected for expressing our needs as children. We may feel again the painful contraction in our bodies, the pressure of unvoiced hurt and sadness that has lain buried deep inside us all these years.

Bringing loving awareness to our own pain is essential if we want to be good leaders to our children and to others. Compassion for one's own suffering is, in fact, the first and most important step in creating a humane, peaceful and just world for everyone. Deep, non-judging self-awareness leads to self-forgiveness, which in turn leads to relaxation and healing. We begin to give ourselves the love we've been needing all along. This non-resisting self-acceptance allows us finally to accept others, including our children. Once we let the clenched fist of unresolved grief relax its hold we begin to notice that others around us are suffering too, and that they need our kindness and compassion. Able at last to love ourselves, we become capable of loving others. True charity, as they say, begins at home.

Chapter Nineteen
The Emptying Nest

Do not kiss your children so they will kiss you back but so they will kiss their children, and their children's children.[42]

Noah benShea

It's been four years now since my youngest child left home for good. I still remember vividly the day I borrowed my sister-in-law's van and helped transport Julia and her belongings to Vancouver. She was going to move into a big heritage house near Chinatown with six other students. It was late spring. She planned to work for the summer and go to college in the fall.

We had a wonderful day together setting up house, buying sheets and light bulbs and hanging her paintings in her room. Then it came time for me to leave. I smiled bravely, hugged her goodbye and headed for the ferry back to Mayne Island. Once on board I climbed into the back of the empty van and lay down on the floor. I burst into uncontrollable sobs. I think the van must have rocked visibly with the vibration of my grief. I cried the whole way home.

It was a clean, deep, pure sadness. I wasn't worried at all about Julia; I knew she was very strong and that she would do just fine without me. I had no regrets about our relationship. We had a bond that could not be broken no matter how far apart we were geographically. I was just filled up to overflowing with a powerful sense both of loss and of beauty. An era was ending. My children, who had once so depended on me, had grown beyond my embrace. They would still love me and I them. But we would never again be as intertwined in each others' lives as we had been.

As I wept in the back of the van a memory resurfaced. I recalled a moment, twenty-three years earlier, when I'd had a similar bittersweet awareness of the passage of time. Lauren was about eight or nine months old. We were at the park, having a picnic on the grass. I was holding her by the waist, helping her balance on her wobbly legs. She was facing away from me and was so delighted by the spectacle of children playing tag on the grass nearby that her whole body vibrated with excitement.

I was powerfully aware at that moment that this would always be my role with respect to her: to stand behind and watch as she reached away from me towards the world. I was her starting place, her balance point from which she would take her first steps. Always out, always away, farther and farther, until one day she would be gone.

I understood clearly then that the parental gaze is exactly this looking at the child who is (and should be) looking away at the world. It is the gaze of one who loves unconditionally, without need or expectation. We fall in love with our babies when they are born, and they love us in return intensely and dependently for a time. But if they are to grow up to be healthy and strong and self-sufficient, they must eventually seek the world beyond us. We have to let them go.

I have let my children go. We are still very great friends. We are still intimate witnesses of each other's life stories even though we don't see each other all the time. My daughters are some of my best supporters, encouraging me enthusiastically in my creative work, listening to me when I am troubled or discouraged. I hope I do the same for them.

I am glad, however, that I gave myself that hour or two of pure, unalloyed grief on the ferry the night my youngest child left home. I am glad I gave heart space to my sense of loss.

Life hurts. Change is challenging. As each new chapter of our personal life story begins, another is ending forever. We have to acknowledge that pain. If we open to life's sadness we stay loose and resilient. I cried so hard I felt purged when I arrived home. Drained. Emptied out. I didn't need to cry anymore. I felt ready to welcome the adventure of the rest of my life.

Afterword
Some Abiding Questions

We are all longing to go home to some place we have never been — a place half-remembered and half-envisioned we can only catch glimpses of from time to time. Community. Somewhere, there are people to whom we can speak with passion without having the words catch in our throats. Somewhere a circle of hands will open to receive us, eyes will light up as we enter, voices will celebrate with us whenever we come into our own power. Community means strength that joins our strength to do the work that needs to be done. Arms to hold us when we falter. A circle of healing. A circle of friends. Someplace where we can be free.[43]

Starhawk

My journey over the past twenty-seven years as a parent has been guided by instinct. I haven't always known where I was headed. At each stage I have just tried to move closer to what felt right and true — like a traveller in a storm drawn towards a distant light. I feel sure now that the "light" that gives warmth and purpose to life is human connection; I believe that we desperately need to redesign our societies so that they nurture our potential for intimacy, mutuality and love instead of forcing us to compete with one another. A win/lose paradigm is unsustainable, both psychologically and ecologically, for us all.

I know where my heart longs to go but I don't know exactly how to get there. I made a small step forward by saying no to the coercive, competitive paradigm underlying "school." But at times I have walked a lonely path. I often longed for that village it takes to raise a child, that community of like-minded people who encourage, inspire and support each other through good times and bad. I have wondered how to find or make such a village and hope that my own children discover it somehow.

Evolution takes time. I know that there are currently many imaginative, courageous people out there who are working hard to re-envision our way of inhabiting the world. I also know that human beings are never going to come up with a "perfect" design for society. Life is messy and organic. The world around us is constantly changing. All structures collapse eventually. What we can do, however, is set a clear intention that will guide our search for solutions, an intention that will hold fast as the solutions change from situation to situation and from one generation to another.

Our intention could be simply this: *the cornerstone of social life will be radical respect*. The highest aim of our institutions, laws and traditions will be to foster loving, mutually respectful relationships between all members of the community and between the human world and the larger ecosystem that sustains it.

What would a society look like that was guided by this fundamental intention? I don't know. I have no answers or solutions, only questions.

1) Would such a society have schools for children? If so, what would they look like?

If schools existed in a loving, radically respectful society, they could never, under any circumstances, be compulsory. No form of coercion, grading, ranking, testing or official competition would be acceptable. Students would participate of their own free will, if and when they chose. Hierarchies of power, status or privilege would make absolutely no sense at all.

How would such non-compulsory schools be paid for? Through taxation? Through pay-as-you-go fees? How would we keep such places of learning accessible to all regardless of income?

What would go on inside the walls of such schools? Would these places of learning look like colleges or community centres, where various courses are on offer during specific sessions? Or would they simply be facilities where the public could come and go, where all had free access to tools and workshops, to books, art supplies, science labs, sports equipment, or whatever else the community chose to offer? Would everyone in the community be invited to share their knowledge, or would specially trained people be hired by the community to "teach" others?

2) What is the role of "work" in a loving society?

Mothers have often said to me, "I would love to homeschool my children, but I have to work in order to pay the mortgage." Many fathers, too, including my own husband, express deep regret that they were not able to spend more time with their young children. Life passes so quickly. After a lifetime of working, many parents find they have all the material comforts they could wish for. But the children have grown up and left. Those precious years when they were still young and eager to be with us are gone forever.

A world in which adults spend most of their waking hours apart from their children is not one that puts relationships first. Such a world values material possessions and social status over intimacy. I would argue that the citizens of such a world inevitably suffer from depression and loneliness, despite their houses and cars and TV sets, because they have neglected their relationships. Love takes time and energy and commitment. A few tired minutes at the end of a long day just isn't enough to sustain a deep and satisfying connection with another human being.

How could we reorganize society so that work and life were less separate? How could we arrange things so that children and parents weren't deprived of each other's company for so many hours of the day? Perhaps we need to ratchet down our desire for material possessions so that earning enough money to "make ends meet" doesn't take such a big bite out of life. Perhaps we need to do more sharing of our resources so that each household isn't obliged to own all their own appliances and tools, for instance.

In traditional tribal societies, child care is shared by many. As well as their parents, children have grandparents, aunts and uncles, cousins and neighbours to help them grow and learn. What changes could we make to our current living arrangements so that we could all share both in the work of survival and in the raising of the children in our communities?

3) Would a loving society be so fixated on being "elsewhere"?

Our current society is in love with media. Most people in our world today spend the bulk of their time inhabiting the virtual worlds presented or facilitated by different media. Chatting on Facebook, playing video games, watching TV, surfing the Internet are forms of "elsewhere addiction." Even reading books is a form of being somewhere else than in the present moment. The danger is that we cease to live in our bodies. We cease to be aware of the rhythms of the natural world around us. We can miss out on real-time relationships with others.

Intimacy involves a capacity for presence. We need to *notice* our surroundings. I wonder whether a culture that encouraged unconditional love and respect for all life would be so enamoured of "representing" the world via media rather than directly experiencing it through our bodies and senses. Would such a culture push the "three Rs" on young children as we do, for instance — causing them to leave off playing outdoors in the fields and parks and forests in favour of sitting passively in front of books and computer screens?

I myself love books and use the computer daily. I don't know what to make of the extent to which media dominate my life. I only want us to think carefully and consciously about their impact on our health. Perhaps, like chocolate or cheese, they are fine in moderation, but need regulating for optimum well-being. Would a life-affirming, earth-honouring culture find ways to protect its children from early over-exposure to media?

4) What is the relationship between work, child-rearing and food?

Ecologists and environmentalists are thinking a lot these days about our relationship with food. To live sustainably, we have to stop transporting food over great distances. We also have to stop growing food in ways that are destructive to the earth. Furthermore, once we embrace a society that radically respects and honours all its citizens, we may find we can no longer engage in practices which so deeply disrespect other forms of life on this planet. We may no longer feel entitled to enslave and torture animals, for instance, just because we like the taste of their flesh.

The "eat locally" movement mirrors for me the "life-learning" movement. Children thrive on the five-mile learning diet; they need access to their local community and to their unique ecological environment, and flourish when they spend time with people who love them and who live right alongside them. Having "professionals" teach and raise our children according to a standardized system designed by strangers seems to me akin to "agro-biz" — it's processed, mass-produced food versus a local, organic diet. It's the monocrop versus biodiversity. Top-down, centralized, one-size-fits-all thinking, whether it comes to food or to education, dangerously ignores the unique microclimate of each family and community.

Perhaps bringing the growing and production of our food back to our communities will help us bring our kids home. Children have always thrived on farms where the work of survival was not segregated from the rest of life and where they grew up intimately familiar with the rhythms of nature. They do best in families that gather together over daily, nourishing meals, where lingering in conversation is more important than rushing to the TV. Perhaps when we begin to be more aware of how our food is grown and to honour the earth it comes from, we will want to treat children with the same tenderness and respect.

5) How would we make collective decisions in a society that holds radical respect of others as its paramount value?

There are traditional societies that have practiced true democracy. Some First Nations, for instance, have traditionally made decisions only through consensus. In such cultures all are invited to speak and to share their opinions and ideas. All are heard. Decisions require much discussion, negotiation and patience and are never made quickly. Only when everyone agrees, sometimes after weeks or months or years of discussion, is a change made. No "chief" or president or autocratic leader is entitled to unilaterally decide for all.

Real democracy is difficult and time-consuming. And it is perhaps, like food and education, best practiced at a local level. I don't know what social contract would be best suited to foster a respectful, loving society, but I know that we need to work on designing one. The current hierarchical, centralized political entities *seem* impressively effective: they are able to make quick, sweeping decisions at the drop of a hat — to go to war, for instance, or to build an oil pipeline through a vast tract of wilderness, or to promote a new miracle drug despite the risk of side effects. But are big, quick decisions always the best ones? We have empowered our governments to bring the earth to the brink of environmental collapse in just a couple of centuries. Whose interest has been served by so much change, so fast?

Can we come up with a better way of making choices? Again, we will have to think hard about what intention should guide our collective decision-making. Currently our societies tend to put "economic growth" and "national security" at the top of the priority list. What if, instead, all our decisions were responses to this primary question: How can we best share this small earth kindly, lovingly and respectfully with all who dwell here with us?

Notes

1. Mary Haskell, *I Care About Your Happiness: Quotations from the Love Letters of Kahlil Gibran and Mary Haskell* (Boulder, CO: Blue Mountain Arts, 1976).

2. Lao Tsu, *Tao Te Ching: A Book about the Way and the Power of the Way*, translated by Ursula K. Le Guin (Shambhala Publications, 1997).

3. Muriel Strode, *My Little Book of Life*, (1912; repr. Nabu Press, 2010).

4. Joseph Campbell, *Reflections on the Art of Living: A Joseph Campbell Companion*, edited by Diane K. Osbon (New York: HarperCollins, 1991), 77.

5. Campbell, Ibid., 79.

6. Thomas Merton, *No Man Is an Island* (Orlando: Harcourt, 1955).

7. Alfie Kohn, *Punished by Rewards: The Trouble with Gold Stars, Incentive Plans, A's, Praise, and Other Bribes* (1993; repr. Boston: Houghton Mifflin, 1999).

8. Kohn, "The Risks of Rewards" (online article), *ERIC (Educational Resource Information Center) Digest*, December 1994, www.ericdigests.org

9. Kohn, "Five Reasons to Stop Saying 'Good Job!'" (online article), *Young Children*, September 2001, http://alfiekohn.org/articles.htm.

10. A.S. Neill, *Summerhill School: A New View of Childhood* (1960; New York: St. Martin's Griffin, 1992), 135.

11. John Taylor Gatto, *Dumbing Us Down: The Hidden Curriculum of Compulsory Schooling* (New Society Publishers, 1992).
12. Woodrow Wilson, quoted in John Taylor Gatto, *Weapons of Mass Instruction: A Schoolteacher's Journey through the Dark World of Compulsory Schooling* (New Society Publishers, 2010).
13. General Education Board, in Occasional Letter Number One (1906), quoted in John Taylor Gatto, *The Underground History of American Education: A Schoolteacher's Intimate Investigation into the Problem of Modern Schooling* (Oxford Village Press, 2003), chapter two.
14. Wendy Priesnitz, "Education Without Coercion" (published on blog), *Education Revolution*, www.educationrevolution.org
15. Priesnitz, "A Life of Learning," Ibid.
16. Grace Llewellyn, *The Teenage Liberation Handbook: How to Quit School and Get a Real Life and Education* (Lowry House, 1998), 40.
17. Marshall Rosenberg, *Nonviolent Communication: A Language of Life* (Encinitas, CA: PuddleDancer Press, 2003), 23.
18. Dawna Markova, *I Will Not Die an Unlived Life: Reclaiming Purpose and Passion* (Emeryville, CA: Conari Press, 2000).
19. Lily Tomlin, quoted in *People* magazine, December 26, 1977.
20. John Holt, *Learning All The Time* (Reading, MA: Perseus Books, 1989), 42.
21. Johan Huizinga, *Homo Ludens: A Study of the Play Element in Culture* (Beacon Press, 1955).
22. Attributed to Mark Twain in *Outing: sport, adventure, travel, fiction* 50 (1907), edited by Caspar Whitney.
23. Widely attributed to the Dalai Lama XIV.
24. Jiddu Krishnamurti, *Talks and Dialogues* (Saanen, 1967).
25. George Sage, "American Values and Sport: Formation of a Bureaucratic Personality," *Journal of Physical Education and Recreation,* October 1978.
26. Alfie Kohn, *No Contest: The Case Against Competition* (New York: Houghton Mifflin, 1992), 85.
27. John Holt, *Freedom and Beyond* (Heinemann Educational Books, 1995), 249.

28. Marie Curie, quoted in Melvin A. Benarde, *Our Precarious Habitat* (W.W. Norton, 1973), v.

29. Albert Einstein, quoted in Matthew Kelly, *The Rhythm of Life: Living Every Day with Passion & Purpose* (1999; New York: Beacon Publishing, 2004), 80.

30. Ken Robinson, TED talk: "Do Schools Kill Creativity?" 2006.

31. Heraclitus of Ephesus (c. 535–475 B.C.), widely quoted, source uncertain.

32. Susan Scarf Merrell, *The Accidental Bond: How Sibling Connections Influence Adult Relationships* (New York: Ballantine Books, 1995), 8.

33. Erich Fromm, *The Art of Loving* (1956; Perennial Classics Edition, 2000), 7.

34. Stephen Levine and Ondrea Levine, *Embracing the Beloved: Relationship as a Path of Awakening* (First Anchor Books, 1996), 135.

35. Henri-Frédéric Amiel, *The Journal Intime of Henri-Frédéric Amiel*, translated by Mary Ward (Macmillan and Co, 1885), 437.

36. Stephen Jenkinson, *How It All Could Be: A Work Book for Dying People and for Those Who Love Them* (Orphan Wisdom, www.orphanwisdom.com), audiobook.

37. Wallace Stevens, "Sunday Morning" (1915).

38. John Welwood, *Toward a Psychology of Awakening: Buddhism, Psychotherapy, and the Path of Personal and Spiritual Transformation* (Shambhala, 2002).

39. Carl Jung, "The Philosophical Tree" (1945). Reprinted in *CW 13: Alchemical Studies*, 335.

40. Naomi Aldort, "Babies & Toddlers: To Tame or to Trust" (online article), www.naomialdort.com.

41. Rosenberg, *Nonviolent Communication*.

42. Noah benShea, *Jacob the Baker: Gentle Wisdom for a Complicated World* (New York: Ballantine Books, 1990).

43. Starhawk, *Dreaming the Dark: Magic, Sex and Politics* (New York: Beacon Press, 1982), 92.

Lauren and Lael, 1985

Lauren, Richard and Marlise, 1990

Lauren, Julia, and Marlise, 1991

Lauren, Marlise and unicorns, 1991

Family Portrait, 1993

Lauren riding her grandmother's horse Pelley, 1995

Marlise reading to Julia, 1996

The three girls drawing, 1996

The girls sunbathing on the sandstone rocks in Campbell Bay, 1996

Our new house

Getting the Christmas tree from the forest, 1998

Marlise kissing Halo, 1999

Julia managing to bottle-feed both 'Coolio' and 'Flicka' at the same time!, 1999

Rasta gets a thorough grooming from Lauren, Marlise, and their friends Emily and Hannah Carr, 1999

Girls with lambs, 1999

The house we built, with the garden growing in

The Iredale Cousins: Meg, Lauren, Julia, Ben, Brody, Ryley, Marlise, and Adam, 2001

Adam, Marlise and Lauren busking at the Saturday Farmer's market on Mayne Island, 2005

The First May Day in our field. The following year it became an island event
in our local park, involving several hundred people, 2005

Julia and Lael on the Camino trail in Southern France, 2008

Marlise performing at Cafe Kona in Calgary, 2010

Julia, Lauren and Marlise at Lauren's wedding, 2010

On a Kayak camping trip from Mayne Island to Cabbage Island, 2012

Julia at work

Marlise and Lael clowning around on May Day, 2013

Looking towards Campbell Bay from our dining room window

Marlise, pregnant Lauren, Richard, Julia, Lael (The three on the left are wearing Inkspoon!), 2013

Index

A

acceptance, unconditional, xvi, 151, 157, 172
adolescence and puberty, 109–10
advice, xviii, 155, 170
Aldort, Naomi, 165–66
Amiel, Henri-Frédéric, 143
anxiety, xvi, xviii, 84, 107–8, 127, 151, 167–68, 171–72
arithmetic, 86–87
art, wearable, 87, 91–93
art and artists, 114, 132
   See also Iredale, Julia: artist; Iredale, Lauren: silk-screen designs; Iredale, Marlise: musician, poet, performer
art as commodity, 161–62
athletics, organized. *See* sports, organized
attention, focused, 112
attention deficit disorder, 9, 113
attention seeking, 168–69

Avatar (movie), 24
awareness
   of children's needs, 163, 165–66, 167
   compassionate, 23, 172
   of death, 146
   respectful, xix
   of self, 107–8, 110, 127, 172
   social, 98
   tension and, 156–57

B

balance, a life in, 61, 93
benShea, Noah, 173
Berklee School of Music, 124
birth order, 131–34
boredom, 117–21
brain, changing the, 112
bribery, 16–18
bullying, 36–42, 96–97
busy-ness, 121, 125, 129

C

Campbell, Joseph, 11–13, 76–77
Campbell Bay Music Festival,

97–98
Canadian Green Building
 Council, 53
Carr, Emily and Hannah, 92g
change, 1, 23, 39–42, 44, 92,
 175
childhood
 birth order, 131–34
 and busy-ness, 121, 125–26,
  129
 criticism, during, 23, 42,
  172
 emotional content of, 62
 existential angst, 129,
  152–55
 and the inner voice, 60–61
 open-ended, 129–30
children('s)
 emotional environment, xv
 emotional well-being, 151,
  156–57
 feeling safe, xvi, 23, 85, 96,
  105, 156–57, 165–66
 labeling, 83
 needs, meeting, xix, 29,
  163–70
 and relationships, xix
choice, 43–44, 52, 63, 170–71
coercion, xi, xviii, 19, 30–31,
 178
college, getting into, 88,
 111–12
communication, nonviolent,
 37–38, 171–72
community/communities, xvi,
 xvii–xviii, 33–34, 177–78

compassion, xv, 23, 95, 106,
 140, 170, 172
compassionate listening, 114,
 156
competition/competitiveness,
 101
 a paradigm of, 64, 90
 in school, 161, 177
 sibling, 131–34
 in sports, 101–6
 uneasy with, 19–20
compulsion schooling, 27
connection, xix, 19, 24, 42,
 53, 177–78
consumerism, 166–67
cooperation, 98
creativity/creative process
 and boredom, 118–22
 a cultural priority, 90–94
 and early childhood
  experiences, xv, xix
 fear of criticism and, 85
 fostering, 84–85
 work, 160–62
culture, re-evaluating, 1,
 11–12, 94, 98–99, 125–29,
 145–46, 161
Curie, Marie, 107
curiosity, 63, 66–67
curricula and content, 29–31,
 63–71

D
Daemon, Marley (Julia
 Iredale), 69
Dalai Lama, 95, 126

de-schooling. See Holt, John: unschooling and unschoolers

death and dying, 21, 108–9, 145–47

decision-making, 43–44, 182

Depersonalization Disorder, 143–45

discipline, 42

disempowerment See empowerment/ disempowerment

dissociation, 142–45

see also Iredale, Julia: existential crisis; Iredale, Lauren; Iredale, Marlise

divergent thinking, 113

domination societies. See societies

Dragonsong (McCaffrey), 82

Dumbing Us Down and *Weapons of Mass Instruction: A Schoolteacher's Journey through the Dark World of Compulsory Schooling* (Gatto), 26

dyslexia/disabled, 83

E

education, 81

alternative and unorthodox, 4–5, 18, 28–31

higher, access to, 88, 111–12

not the central issue, xv–xvi

the old paradigm, questioning, 15–24,

29–30, 64, 90, 177–82

See also public schools

education at home. *See* homeschooling and homeschoolers

educators, 30, 64

Einstein, Albert, 111

Elfquest (Pini), 66

"elsewhere addiction," 180

Emily Carr Institute of Art and Design, 67–68, 89, 91

empathy, 23, 98, (add) 169

empowerment/ disempowerment, 35–36, (add) 79

emptying nest, 173–75

existential angst and crises See dissociation; Iredale, Julia: an existential crisis

Expressive Arts Therapy, 69

F

family, extended, 55–57

fear, xvi, 26, 43, 85, 102, 129, 151

feelings, 38, 60–62, 130, 149, 155–56

Fish and Bird (band), 97–98

Flaubert, Gustave, 2

food, relationship with, 90, 166, 181

Forestorium (secret world), 56

freedom

to explore and learn, 31, 36, 90–94, 159–60

and fathers, 125–26

in journaling, 109–10
a month off work, 129–30
the outsider's, 128
to play, 74–79
Starhawk's, 177
Fromm, Erich, 135

G
Gatto, John Taylor, 26–30, 38
genius, ordinary, xiii, 111–15
globalization, 90, 94
Gray, Peter (brother-in-law),
    21, 55–56
grief, 35, 120, 145–47, 157,
    171–72

H
Haskell, Mary, xv
hearts, our, 130, 141, 156–
    57, 171
Heraclitus of Ephesus, 117
heroic journey, the, 11–13
hierarchy. *See* societies
Holt, John, 9–11, 65, 105
    unschooling and
        unschoolers, 30–32, 111–
        14, 124–25, 130, 181
homeschooling alliance, xi–xii
homeschooling and
    homeschoolers
    the 3 R's, 65, 81–88, 127
    and boredom, 117–21
    bribery, 16–18
    creative writing, 84–85, 107
    and creativity, 57, 118–22
    and friends, 11, 56–57, 101

the journal, 107–10
learning skills, 65, 83–87,
    107, 112
and loneliness, 52, 128
outsiders, 62, 128
proficiency tests, 88
Qs & As about, 179–80
supplies, 15–16
See also Iredale, Julia;
    Iredale, Lauren; Iredale,
    Marlise; Whitehead,
    Lael; Whitehead, Lael,
    journals
horses, 6, 46–49, 70–71
Huizinga, Johan, 73

I
imagination, creative, 32–33,
    66–69, 144, 159–60, 167
Inkspoon (wearable art
    company), 87, 89, 91–93
interests and talents, 32, 63,
    68–70, 98, 112–15, 131–
    34, 167
intimacy, 42, 107, 147, 177,
    180
Iredale, Ben, Rylan and
    Brodey (nephews), 55–57,
    92h
Iredale, Jennifer (sister-in-
    law), 55–56
Iredale, Julia (daughter), 92b–
    h, 140b, 140e, 140f, 140h
    artist, 67–68, 87, 114, 132,
        154, 160–62
    birth and birth order, 3,

131–34
an existential crisis, 152–55
journaling, 67, 109–10, 132
leaving home, 173–74
her perspective, 159–62
permission to tell her story,
    xvii
personality, 16, 133
reader and writer, 81–85
sexual awakening, 139
traveler, 67–68, 155
See also Mayne Island, the
    move to
Iredale, Lauren (daughter),
    92a–e, 92g–h, 140a,
    140c–e, 140h
an alternative community,
    xvii–xviii
birth and birth order, 1–3,
    131–34
bullied, 36–37, 171
dissociation, 144–45
grandfather, relationship
    with, 39–42
high school, 57, 90–91, 136
homeschooling, 11, 13,
    15–18
permission to tell her story,
    xvii
her perspective, 89–94
public school, aversion to,
    5–9, 11, 36, 59–60, 92
reader, writer, designer,
    entrepreneur, 66–67, 81,
    84, 114, 121
sexual encounter, first,

135–36, 140
silk-screen designs, 66, 87,
    91–93
See also Mayne Island, the
    move to
Iredale, Marlise (daughter),
    92a–h, 140a–b, 140e,
    140g
birth and birth order, 3,
    131–34
dissociation, 144–45
her perspective, 123–30
high school, 57
home schooling, 15–17,
    124–30
journaling, 108–9
musician, poet and
    performer, 53–55, 68–70,
    75–76, 81, 114, 124
permission to tell her story,
    xvii
personality, 132, 133
reading, 82–83
sexual encounter, first,
    135–40
the sleep over, 163–64
world traveler, 123
writer, 57, 84, 119
See also Mayne Island, the
    move to
Iredale, Rand (father-in-law),
    39–42
Iredale, Richard (husband),
    92a, 92c, 8–9, 11, 31, 55,
    81–82, 101, 112, 140h
dissociation, 142–43

early married life, 1–3
goal oriented, 125–26
and his daughters, 59–60,
    62, 70–71, 77–78, 86–87,
    137–38, 152, 166–67
his inner voice, 59–62
the money earner, 12,
    125–26
stress level, reducing his,
    44–49, 53
Iredale, Tab and Paddy
    (brother- and sister-in-law),
    55–56
Iredale-Gray, Adam (nephew),
    54, 55–57, 92h, 97–98,
    112, 140a
Iredale-Gray, Meg (niece),
    55–57, 82, 92h

J
Jackie (babysitter), 36–37, 171
Jacques, Brian, 82–83
Jaiya (Celtic-jazz trio), 54
Jenkinson, Stephen, 145–46
journaling. See under Iredale,
    Julia; Iredale, Marlise;
    Whitehead, Lael, journals
judgment
    and compassion, 23
    and creativity, 90–91, 93
    and feeling safe, 156
    in human development,
        114–15
    leadership and, 165–66,
        171–72
    meeting needs and, 169

and power, 37–38
in schools, 5, 28, 84
thriving and, xvi
Jung, Carl, 163

K
Karen and Ken (friends), 50
kindness, 98
knowledge versus curriculum,
    63–65
Kohn, Alfie, 18–19, 33,
    78–79, 104–6
Krishnamurti, Jiddu, 101

L
labelling, 83–84, 115
language, 37–38
Lao Tsu, xvii
leadership, parental, 163–72
learning
    the basic assumption about,
        15–17
    communities, 33–34
    enough, 26
    from experience, 60–62,
        140
    and love, xv–xvi
    many ways of, 29–31,
        64–66
    social skills, 4–5, 95–99
    at their own pace, 11
    through journaling, 107–10
    through play, 73–79
    without schooling, xi–xii,
        81–88
Levine, Stephen, 141

life and lifestyle, xvi, 23, 43,
  107, 178
  a call to, 11–13
  choosing a, 43–58, 75,
    159–60, 162
  designing a, 89–94
  by instinct, 177–78
  questioning, 117–22,
    124–29, 141–47
  suffering and pain in,
    150–56, 171–72, 175
  work and, 179–81
  see also Rosenberg, Marshall
life-force, 13
life-learning. See Holt, John:
  unschooling and
  unschoolers
Life Learning Magazine, 28
literacy, 84
Llewellyn, Grace, 35
loneliness/aloneness, 12, 52,
  62, 110, 128, 154, 177–78
love and loving, 15, 98, 135,
  177
  death and, 146–47
  and education, xv–xvi
  giving and withholding,
    155–57
  leadership, 163–72
  and learning, xix–xx
  relationships, 24
  romantic, 136, 140
  unconditional, 156–57, 174

M
Markova, Dawna, 43

Marvin (friend), 141, 143,
  145, 147
math, 16–17, 86–87
Mayne Island
  the move to, 43–58, 61, 85
  the house and the view,
    92e, 92h, 140h
  kayaking, 140f
  May Day, 140a
McCaffrey, Anne, 82
media, in love with, 180
Merrell, Susan Scarf, 131
Merton, Thomas, 15, 24
Michelle (friend), 54, 68–69,
  163–64
Mormon culture, 20, 21
motivation, intrinsic and
  extrinsic, xi, 18–19, 78
music and musicians, 53–55,
  57, 69–70, 75–76,
  97–98, 112
  See also Iredale, Marlise:
    musician, poet and
    performer

N
natural-learning. See Holt,
  John: unschooling and
  unschoolers
Natural Life Magazine, xi, 28
Neill, A.S., 25
No Contest: The Case Against
  Competition (Kohn), 104
Nonviolent Communication: A
  Language of Life (Rosenberg),
  37–38

O

outside the box, thinking, 113

outsiders, 59, 62, 97, 128

P

pain and suffering, 23, 96, 149–51, 171–72

paradigms, cultural, 37–39, 128

paradigms, educational, 15–24, 25–34, 64, 90, 177–78

parenting, xii, 9, 163–72, 177

passions. *see* interests and talents

Peter (friend), 21

Pini, Wendy, 66

play and playfulness
imaginative, 68–70
learning through, 73–79
letting children, 25–26, 32–33
organized sports and, 104
and socialization, 99
and work, 74–77, 91

potential, fulfilling their, 71, 94, 115

power, 13
the language of, 35–42
of public schools, 27–31
relationships, 20–21

practice time, 75–76

Priesnitz, Wendy, xi–xiii (forward), 28–29

productivity obsession, 125–26

puberty and adolescence, 109–10

public schools, 35
adult-child ratio in, 98–99
applying for college, 88, 111–12
critics of, 26–29, 38
dislike of, 98–99 (*See also* Iredale, Lauren: public school, an aversion to)
and divergent thinking, 113
of the future, 94, 177–179
and socialization, 95–99
See also education

Punished by Rewards: the Trouble with Gold Stars, Incentive Plans, A's, Praise and Other Bribes (Kohn), 18

Q

Qi (life force), 13

R

radical respect, xvi, xix–xx, 29–30, 31, 42, 178–82

Raffi (Raffi Cavoukian), 54

reading, 81–84

Redwall series (Jacques), 82–83, 84

relationships
adversarial, 104–6
fostering, xvi
radically respectful, xix–xx, 42, 178

seeing, 24
and sexuality, 140
the starting place, xv–xvi
unequal power, 19, 20–21,
23, 37, 39–42
who we are, 96
and working parents,
179–80
relaxation, 156–57, 169
resistance, 156
respect. *See* radical respect
rewards and punishments,
xviii, 16–20
Riesman, David, 104
right and wrong (moral grey
areas), 108–9
Roaring Jelly (band), 54
Robinson, Ken, 113, 114–15
Rockefeller, John D., 27–28
Rosenberg, Marshall, 37–38,
171–72

S
Sage, George, 104, 106
Sandberg, Mischa, 36
self-esteem, 126
sexuality, 21–22, 135–40
sheep farmers, 50–51, 108–9
siblings, 131–34
silk-screening, 91–92
skills. *See* homeschooling and
homeschoolers: learning
skills
socialization, 95–99, 104
societies, 27–29, 37–39, 90,
104, 160–61, 177–82

song and dance, 53–54
space and spaciousness, 44,
91, 127–30
spelling, 16–17, 84–86, 109
sports, organized, 101–6
Star Wars (movie), 60–61
Starhawk (Miriam Simos),
160, 177
Stevens, Wallace, 146–47
Strode, Muriel, 1
success, 94, 124
supporters, xvi, 33
sustainably, living, 94, 181

T
talents and interests, 32, 63,
68–70, 98, 112–15, 131–
34, 167
Tamsin (friend), 111–112
tantrums, 165
Teach Your Own (Holt),
9–10, 30–31
teachers and teaching, 15,
26–32, 98–99, 113
TED Talk on Education, 113
television, 166–67
3 Rs, the, 81–88
time, unpressured, 112
time out, xviii, 155–56
tolerance, 98, 109
Tomlin, Lily, 63
tough love approach, 8,
35–36, 42
trust/distrust, 151, 165, 166
Twain, Mark, 81

U

university, getting into, 88, 111–12
unschooling and unschoolers. *see* Holt, John: unschooling and unschoolers

V

value systems, 4, 94, 125, 129, 143, 145–47, 160–62
Vancouver Homelearners' Association, 31–34
verbal airspace, 132–33
Victoria College of Art, 111
virtual world, the, 180
voice, inner, 59–62
void, the, 129–30, 143–44

W

Welwood, John, 149
Whitehead, Lael, 92a, 92c, 140b, 140g–h
    about the book, xv–xvi, xvii–xx
    authors and mentors, 18, 26–27, 28–29, 30–31, 37–38, 104, 113, 143, 147, 165
    early married years, 1–5
    nervous collapse, 61–62
    public schooling to home schooling, 5–13, 15–24, 25–26, 31–34, 35–42
    raising ordinary geniuses, 111–15
    a redesigned society, 177–82

sharing doubts, 141–47
    a win/lose childhood, 19–23
    see also Mayne Island: the move to
Whitehead, Lael, journals
    about journaling, xviii, 107–10
    awakening sexuality, 136–38
    boredom and creativity, 119–20
    dissociation, 144–45
    hamming it up, 68–69
    on horses, 47–48
    Julia, 152–54
    Lauren, 6–7
    on math, 86–87
    the natural world, 52
    on organized sports, 102–3
    on play, 73–74, 77–78
    on reading, 82–83
    on sensitive leadership, 164, 167–68
    when things don't go well, 117–18
Whitehead, Lee and Lorita (parents), 20–23
Whitehead, Paul (brother), 21–22
win/lose ethic, 19, 105, 177
work
    creative, 91, 160–62
    and play, 74–77, 79
    relationship with food, 181
    the role of, 179–80
worry, 150–54

writing, 84–85
Wylder, Blake (Lauren's
husband), 66, 87, 89,
91–94, 140d

Y
Yvette (friend), 54

Z
Zoe (friend), 54

Lael Whitehead is a musician and writer who lives on Mayne Island, BC. Lael performs and records with Jaiya (www.jaiya.ca), Banquo Folk Ensemble (www.banquo.ca) and the Dancehall Players. She has also recently published her first novel for children, *Kaya Stormchild*. Lael and her husband, architect Richard Iredale, raised their three daughters without formal schooling.

Lael is a former editor of BC's *Home Education News* magazine. She has published numerous articles on alternative education, including one recently collected in Wendy Priesnitz's *Life Learning: Lessons from the Educational Frontier*.

Lauren in front of her Inkspoon booth at a festival, 2009

Lauren and Blake's Wedding in the Sheep Field. They are standing on
a five pointed mandala Lauren and Blake created out of natural materials
found on the land — cedar bark, shells, ferns, etc., 2010